www.crossmountainbooks.com/historicalreprint

Cross Mountain Books

engaging books that inform, educate, and inspire

Scan QR code for videos taken
in and around Wolf Creek, Tennessee
(https://tinyurl.com/CMBYouTubeVideos)

Scan QR code for newspaper articles and other time period research
relating to Oblique City and Wolf Creek, Tennessee
(crossmountainbooks.com/oblique-city-resources)

Oblique City, Tennessee.

(Original Title)

Original Cover

Original Inside Cover

Original Title Page Info

PROSPECTUS

OF THE

American Oblique Manufact'g

AND

City Development Co.

INCORPORATED, JUNE 12th, 1893.

(Originally) Published by H. L. MCQUEEN.
WASHINGTON, D. C.

Historical Reprint by

Cross Mountain Books
Valdosta, Georgia
www.crossmountainbooks.com

Published by Cross Mountain Books in Valdosta, Georgia

Manufactured in the United States of America.

First Printing: 1894 by H. L. McQueen as *Oblique City, Tennessee*
Second Printing: 2022 by Cross Mountain Books

Cover Photography © by Andy Peck
    Front: Railroad over French Broad River close to Weaver's Bend (23 Oct 2017)
    Back: Minnehaha Cascade, Wolf Creek Falls, Wolf Creek, TN (18 Feb 2022)

Dedication page photo courtesy of Walker Family

Signed copies available. Books also available in quantity for promotional or premium use. For information, email info@crossmountainbooks.com.

www.crossmountainbooks.com
Facebook: fb.me/crossmountainbooks

Thank you for reading! Please submit a review on your purchase platform.

Publisher's Cataloging-in-Publication Data

Names: American Oblique Manufacturing and City Development Company. | Peck, Andy (Thomas Andrew), 1981- , editor.
Title: Oblique City : Wolf Creek, Tennessee / American Oblique Manufacturing and City Development Company ; edited by Andy Peck.
Description: Valdosta, GA : Cross Mountain Books, 2022. | Series: Historical reprint. | Includes maps, sketches, and photos. | Includes bibliographical references and index. | Summary: Historical reprint of the original 1894 business prospectus seeking to attract investors from around the world in a venture to create a temperance city with manufacturing plants on the French Broad River, a pleasure hotel, and home sites in Wolf Creek, Tennessee.
Identifiers: LCCN 2022910377 | ISBN 9781955121200 (pbk) | ISBN 9781955121217 (hardcover) | ISBN 9781955121224 (ebook)
Subjects: LCSH: Wolf Creek (Tenn.) -- History. | Tennessee, East—History. | Peck family. | Allen family. | Real property -- Tennessee. | Temperance -- United States -- Tennessee. | BISAC: HISTORY / United States / 19th Century. | HISTORY / United States / State & Local / South (AL, AR, FL, GA, KY, LA, MS, NC, SC, TN, VA, WV). | BUSINESS & ECONOMICS / Real Estate / General.
Classification: LCC F442.1 A44 2022| DDC 975 A44--dc23
LC record available at https://lccn.loc.gov/2022910377

Betty,
thank you for sharing your love
of Wolf Creek with me and so many others.
And thank you for your devotion to preserving its history.
~Andy Peck

This historical reprint dedicated to
Ms. Betty (Maricle) Walker of
Wolf Creek, Tennessee
on the occasion of her
92nd birthday

INTRODUCTION

In June 1891, Lewis Washington Murch traveled with J. C. Williamson and G. D. Kennedy to Chicago to test a new process for finishing wood.[1] By April 1892 and most likely well before, Murch was soliciting interested parties to invest in his business venture, "this healthful, picturesque town site, extending for three miles along the French Broad River, which furnishes six large water-powers, giving over 2,500-horse power each, and through which the E. T., V. and G. R[ailwa]y. runs from east to west, and which is watered by the limpid Wolf Creek and two chalybeate springs—and all at the low price of $25 per acre."[2] He had patented his "oblique" wood finishing process, and had grandiose plans to establish a new town called "Oblique City" in Wolf Creek, where his oblique wood could be manufactured.

On 12 June 1893, Murch and his associates filed the charter for their company, the American Oblique Manufacturing and City Development Co. Their stated purpose was to "establish an ideal town, where immorality shall be unknown and gin mills absolutely prohibited."[3] By Sep 1893, Murch was off to Europe to sell stock and "possibly organize another company."[4]

The plans never materialized, Wolf Creek did not turn into Oblique City, no grand hotel or manufacturing plants were ever built, and throughout 1895-1896, a court battle occurred between Cynthia (Allen) Cowan (28 Jun 1817 – Mar 1910) and George Thomas Allen (25 Dec 1871 – 11 Mar 1900) vs. Murch, Clarence H. Steed, and Fred R. Carver. Tennessee Supreme Court records reveal that the defendants, Murch et. al, were required to sell back the lands they had purchased from Cowan and Allen.

Wolf Creek is still a small, quiet community that sits along the beautiful French Broad River in Cocke County, Tennessee. Wolf Creek's clear water continues to quietly flow around its mountain homes. My research has revealed little of what became of Murch, his associates, and the Oblique Manufacturing Company.

I am grateful to Ms. Betty Walker of Wolf Creek for sharing *Oblique City* with me. This document contains treasures about the Peck family, but also many others in and around this area. I have added the index to help everyone discover more about this community, its families, and our past.

~Andy Peck

---

[1] The Dickinson Press (Dickinson, ND), 13 Jun 1891, Pg 3.
[2] Chicago Tribune (Chicago, IL), 10 Apr 1892, Pg 24.
[3] The Journal and Tribune (Knoxville, TN), 13 Jun 1893, Pg 8.
[4] The Dickinson Press (Dickinson, ND), 16 Sep 1893, Pg 3.

PROSPECTUS

OF THE

American Oblique Manufact'g

AND

City Development Co.

INCORPORATED, JUNE 12th, 1893.

Published by H. L. McQUEEN.
WASHINGTON, D. C.

Sectional State Map, Showing Relation of Wolf Creek to Surrounding Country.

Map of French Broad River and Tributaries.

DOWN IN TENNESSEE
(Poem from Oblique City)

To the sweet, sunny South, where so much I delight
    The grand old forests to roam,
Where the mocking birds sing so sweetly at night, —
    To the South we invite you to come.
Come to Wolf Creek and build you a home,
    Where malaria and consumption never are born.

Then come to Wolf Creek. We invite you to come,
Where cyclones and blizzards never are known.

[Dame Nature has,]
With motherly love and care,
    Placed a chalybeate spring close by from which we drink;
And breathing the pure mountain air
    Health is restored.   In truth,
It equals Ponce De Leon's Fount of Youth.

For here 'neath mistletoe and myrtle's lovely green,
    'Neath azure skies where gentle zephyrs fan the cheek,
We'd have a lovely, cozy nook, by mortals seldom seen;
    'T would be a restful haven for weary souls to seek.

CONTENTS.

5

INDEX OF LANDSCAPE VIEWS AND MAPS.

7

C. H. STEAD, Vice-President, Secretary, and Director

F. R. CARVER, Treasurer and Director.

L. W. MURCH, President, General Manager, and Director.

To the sweet, sunny South, where so much I delight
   The grand old forests to roam,
Where the mocking birds sing so sweetly at night,—
   To the South we invite you to come.
Come to Wolf Creek and build you a home,
   Where malaria and consumption never are born.

· WOLF CREEK:

ITS

History and Topography.

SURROUNDED by those lordly old mountains which occupy the southern border of Cocke County, Tennessee,
is a spot of surpassing attractiveness, known as "Wolf
Creek." It takes its name from the sparkling mountain
brook that leaps forth from the bosom of the lofty Walnut
Mountains, and dashes its limpid waters furiously onward
until swallowed up by the mighty French Broad River.
At the confluence of these streams and stretching along the
river a distance of over 3 miles is a tract of land comprising over
450 acres, which is widely known as the Allen farm at "Wolf
Creek." The railroad station is laid down as "Wolf Creek."
It lies 4 miles west of the celebrated "Paint Rock," 10 miles
west of the Hot Springs of North Carolina, and is 47 miles
northwest from Asheville, N. C. It is connected by lines of
railway with the city of Charleston, on the southern seaboard,
and with Cincinnati on the north, being about equidistant,
or 350 miles from each. The French Broad River, which

11

FIG. 1.—Allen Residence at Wolf Creek, Tennessee.

FIG. 2.—Flower Garden in Rear of Allen Residence.

flows along the north border of these lands, is an important tributary of the great Mississippi River, the "Father of waters," and is navigable for boats of light draft to within about 25 miles of Wolf Creek. Some seventy or eighty years ago Reuben Allen, recognizing the advantages and the great resources offered at Wolf Creek, purchased an extensive body of land there, and availing himself of the manifold opportunities that presented themselves, he soon amassed a handsome fortune, which he left to a large and interesting family, some of whom still occupy the old home (see Fig. 1). This is a delightful picture of an enchanting and enjoyable home in the midst of fine trees, shrubbery and flowers, which, together with their variegated foliage, form a lovely scene. There is a beautiful bower in the rear of the grand old place (see Fig. 2); and to add to the attractiveness of this delightful picture we have the limpid creek, and looking south we see Observatory Mountain towering above us in mighty grandeur, perpetually clothed with ever-green verdure. By building an observatory on the top of this grand old mountain we could command an extensive view of a vast stretch of country in every direction, as it towers above the river about 400 feet. We could not get a good view from the top, as it is thickly covered with trees, but got a fine view from the base, showing Deer Park Mountain in the distance (see Fig. 3).

These mountains are the natural home of deer, and are capable of making a fine game park in the near future. Looking south from Lake View Park we get a splendid view of Observatory Mountain (see Fig. 4).

From the southeast corner of Lake View Park we get a fine view up Wolf Creek to the east of Observatory Mountain, with Allen house in view (see Fig. 5).

We will now take up the chain of our history of Mr. Reuben

Allen, and will say it was a most fortunate investment for himself and his descendants, for it proved to be one of those favored spots upon which Nature delights to lavish her successive, ever-increasing, and never-ending favors. First, the productive farm lands, the rich pasturage upon the mountains, the large supply of wild game in the woods, and of fish in the streams; next, the turnpike road, breaking through the barrier that stood between the grain and stock-producing country of East Tennessee and Kentucky, and the cotton-growing States of the South, opened up a thorough-fare for increasing travel for man and live stock, and furnished a home market for the bountiful products of the fertile lands. Following this at a later day came the present line of railway. Nature, still true to her purpose of filling even to overflowing the laps of those at Wolf Creek whom she had so long de-lighted to lavish her gifts upon, seemed to throw across the way for long years an insurmountable barrier beyond which the railroad should not pass, and forced the stopping of the cars, with their human freight, at the very doors of the hospitable country inn. Then, when the cars had passed on, came the delightful summer resort, with every room filled with happy guests, and others knocking and begging admit-tance even if the floors should be their bed. Here again a rich harvest was garnered which made Mr. Allen's investment a most fortunate one. And what next? Can there be any further favors in store for her, or is Nature's supply exhausted? No, she is not weary yet, but rather has in reserve gifts far richer than those she has bestowed. If not, what means that mighty river leaping in wild velocity over these mountain barriers, which plainly tell us she has power. What means these extensive forests of valuable timber, these hills and mountains abounding in profitable ores? What means this extensive and lovely town site, this popular and widely known

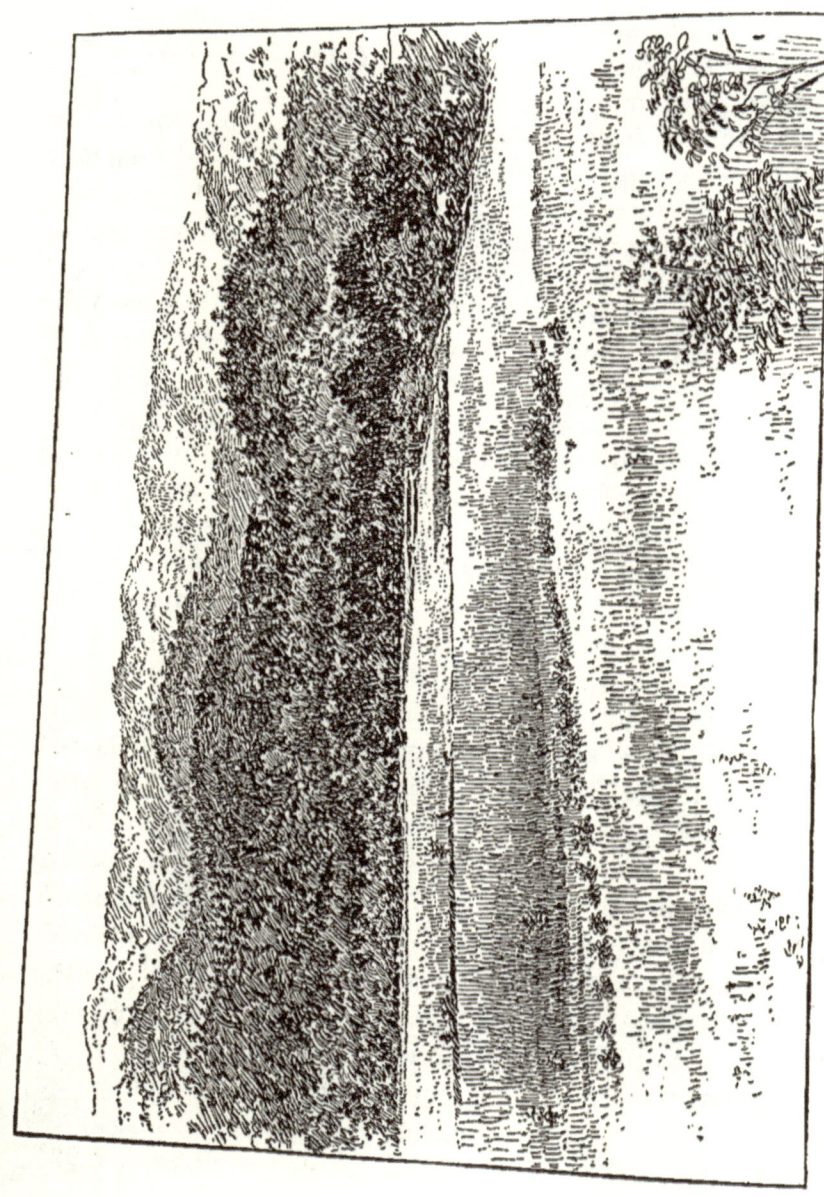

FIG. 3.—Looking North from Observatory Mountain, above Allen Residence, Deer Park Mountain in Distance.

FIG. 4.—Observatory Mountain, as seen from Lake View Park.

FIG. 5.—Looking up Wolf Creek, South from Lake View Park

summer resort, with its pure, bracing air, its health-giving waters, and its opportunities for sport and amusement. No, there is more to come yet, for we see in the near future grand possibilities, and are determined to reap a rich reward from the great opportunities Wolf Creek offers, and plant here a manufacturing city, and health and pleasure resort of no mean proportions, whose corner-stone shall rest upon a strictly moral and temperance base. Years ago that distinguished civil engineer, Major R. C. McCalla, of Tuscaloosa, Alabama, said to Mr. D. W. Allen, of Wolf Creek: "David, there will be a manufacturing city built here some day." The prediction when made may have seemed visionary and scarcely to be hoped for, but now that the foundation is being laid, the Major may live to see his prediction verified, and Wolf Creek, availing herself of the rich treasures laid up for her in Nature's storehouse, shall ere long become the Mountain Queen, and the pride of East Tennessee.

Combining together, as Wolf Creek does, so much of the useful and beautiful, it is plain to see that it should in the near future be made a place of great importance. Such attractions and advantages as those which do exist can not longer lie dormant. She holds in her bountiful hands something for every class of worthy people.

To the shrewd business man she offers opportunities for safe and profitable investment. To the manufacturer she presents her superior water-power, free gifts, cheap labor, and immense forests of useful and valuable timbers of the finest quality. To the tanner she offers ample supplies of the different barks he needs.

As a health and pleasure resort Wolf Creek is a place of unusual natural attractions. The grand mountain scenery, the pure air, the springs of chalybeate, sulphur, and free-stone waters, the beautiful pleasure grounds which can here

19

*word crossed out above: original = "beautiful" / written = "bountiful"

be made, and carriage ways along the river side and into the flower-hedged recesses of the great mountain ranges; the crystal mountain brook with its limpid waters and its speckled trout; that monster lofty peak, the "Bluff," which, like a defiant Goliath, stands out in mighty strength, and lifting his burly head high above the clouds looks down upon his subjects in his own and other States and says to the feeble invalid, "come to me and I will give you strength"; to the weary, "come, for here is peaceful rest for you"; to the lovers of Nature, "come and drink of the health-giving beverage which sparkles at my base." Delightful climate indeed! With its cool summers and mild winters, it offers to the people of the sultry South and the frigid North alike a refuge from the heat to one, from the bitter cold, accompanied by its death-dealing storms and blizzards, to the other.

Then come to Wolf Creek. We invite you to come,
Where cyclones and blizzards never are known.

WOLF CREEK:

ITS

Great Resources and Future Promise

AS A

MANUFACTURING TOWN.

AS coming events cast their shadows before, one can easily predict the brilliant and prosperous future which awaits our proposed city, surrounded and backed up as it is by vast virgin forests of the finest quality of valuable timber in great variety, principally consisting of many kinds of oak and hickory. We have also millions of feet of the finest chestnut, poplar, pine, hemlock (by the natives called spruce pine), maple, black and white birch of the finest quality. Black birch closely resembles mahogany, and is frequently mistaken for cherry by experts.

. The above varieties predominate. We have many other kinds, the principal of which are the beautiful variegated cedar, black and honey locust, ash, beech, walnut, cherry, mulberry, sycamore, holly, fir balsam (by the natives called red fir), the grain of which shows a beautiful purple tinge ; buckeye, a very white and beautiful timber ; and gopher, a beautiful and valuable timber, closely resembling box-wood in color.

To give a clear understanding of this picturesque health and pleasure resort, and its great natural resources, capable of building and sustaining a large manufacturing town, I will briefly explain how my attention was first called to it, and what I have discovered by actual investigation and exploration, the result of which is what I will vouch for as *what I know*, and *is not* based upon mere hearsay.

In the fall of 1891, when looking for a water-power and building site to locate a manufacturing business, Major W. R. Smith, of Newport, Tennessee, called my attention to Wolf Creek as the best place he knew of in the South, undeveloped, as it had a good railroad and the French Broad River running through it, and plenty of backing in its great natural resources to build and maintain a large manufacturing town ; that it was 18 miles from Newport, on the East Tennessee, Virginia and Georgia railway, and the only available spot (with good water-power) between Newport, Tenn., and Asheville, N. C., a distance of 60 miles, to build a large town, and that Wolf Creek had been a favorite health resort for many years. Knowing the Major to be a man of high moral character, on whose *every word* I could rely, I decided to investigate, and accompanied by him I visited Wolf Creek. After putting in a few days in the mountains among the valuable timber, and walking over the old plantations which constitute the town-site, and making a careful estimate of the water-power which the French Broad River would furnish, sufficient to run more than one hundred large factories, I fully agreed with the Major that he had not over-estimated the possibilities of this remarkable location for building a very beautiful and desirable health and pleasure resort, as well as a large manufacturing town.

Nature has here laid the foundation for a wealthy metropolis, and so perfectly has she done her work that the most expert engineer could hardly make any change for the better.

Let us now make a critical review and see if I have over-estimated this valuable and picturesque site and its possibilities. We have 457 acres of choice land in this beautiful valley, surrounded by picturesque mountain scenery which is seldom equaled, lying nicely above and parallel with the crystal waters of the mammoth French Broad River, which runs on the north side, and entirely through our proposed city. The river has sufficient fall from Buffalo Rock on the east boundary to the west end of the site (a distance of over 3 miles) to give ample fall for four dams across the river of 2,500 horse power each, with plenty of flume room and building space to utilize the whole of this immense water power, and ample yard room for each. Then let us take into account another point of great value which "Dame Nature" has so kindly furnished us, which is a low tract of land lying mostly on the south side of the river, and west of Wolf Creek, now covered with timber (see Fig. 6).

Fig. 6.—Birds-Eye View of East Oblique City Site, Looking West from Rock House Mountain.

In Fig. 6 we get a fine view of East Oblique City from the top of Rock House Mountain. In this view we see the timber which is to be cut off, and land covered with water. We call this large body of water Lake View, which will be 4,200 feet long, with an area of nearly 50 acres. On the flat land of Wolf Creek it will flow back a little above the railroad bridge (see map). Then we have a tract of 50 acres of very fine land on the north side of the river which runs nearly down to dam No. 3. We have a fine view of this in Fig. 6.

At the southwest corner of this beautiful lake we have laid out a delightful park, to which we give the very appropriate title of Lake View Park. From this park (which is now covered with corn) can be seen the Oblique Hotel site and neighboring elevated residence lots at base of mountains (see Fig. 7).

Our hotel site is a beautiful elevated mound with an altitude of 100 feet above the river (see Fig. 8). Between fence at foot of hotel site, and second fence next to the railroad will be Oblique Park. Directly in front of this, and between railroad and river (where corn is now growing), is Riverside Park. In this park will be the Passenger Depot (see map).

As can be seen in Fig. 6, which gives a fine view of East Oblique City, we have the great advantage of a railroad running the entire length of the town and parallel with the river, with sufficient mill and yard room (see map) between river and railroad, giving ample room for side tracks to accommodate manufacturers to load and unload direct from their factories to the cars, and *vice versa*, thereby making a great saving in cost of truck work and extra transportation. This is a great point of vantage which manufacturers fully appreciate. As can be seen from our map and Fig. 6, the

24

entire manufacturing part of the town is between the railroad and river, which makes it much more desirable and convenient for the residence part of the town than it would be with the railroad running through the center, and enhances its value (for a city site) to a much greater extent.

We will again call the reader's attention to another very desirable point of vantage, when we speak of a health and pleasure resort, which is our hotel site designated as "Oblique Hotel" (see map and Fig. 8). THIS VERY DESIRABLE AND PICTURESQUE ELEVATION seems to have been chosen by "Dame Nature" as a health and pleasure resort, as she has

With motherly love and care
. Placed a chalybeate spring close by from which we drink ;
And breathing the pure mountain air
Health is restored. In truth,
It equals Ponce De Leon's Fount of Youth.

This beautiful site has an elevation of 100 feet above the level of the river. Here we have a fine view of the grand and picturesque scenery, and the majestic river below, and will be well above and directly in front of our proposed Oblique and Riverside Parks, and Passenger Depot (see Fig. 9), while in the distance we have a grand panoramic view of mountain peaks as they rise one above another in mighty grandeur, a fit object lesson of the wonderful works of an all-wise and Omnipotent God.

Standing where the centre of the front of the hotel will be, by exact measurement it is 150 yards to the chalybeate spring (see map). Aside from this health-giving spring we have two fine mountain springs of pure, cold water (one on each side of this charming elevation) which come from the mountain in the background, and meander down to the river below. These fine springs are plentiful on this side of the mountains the entire length of the town, making it an easy

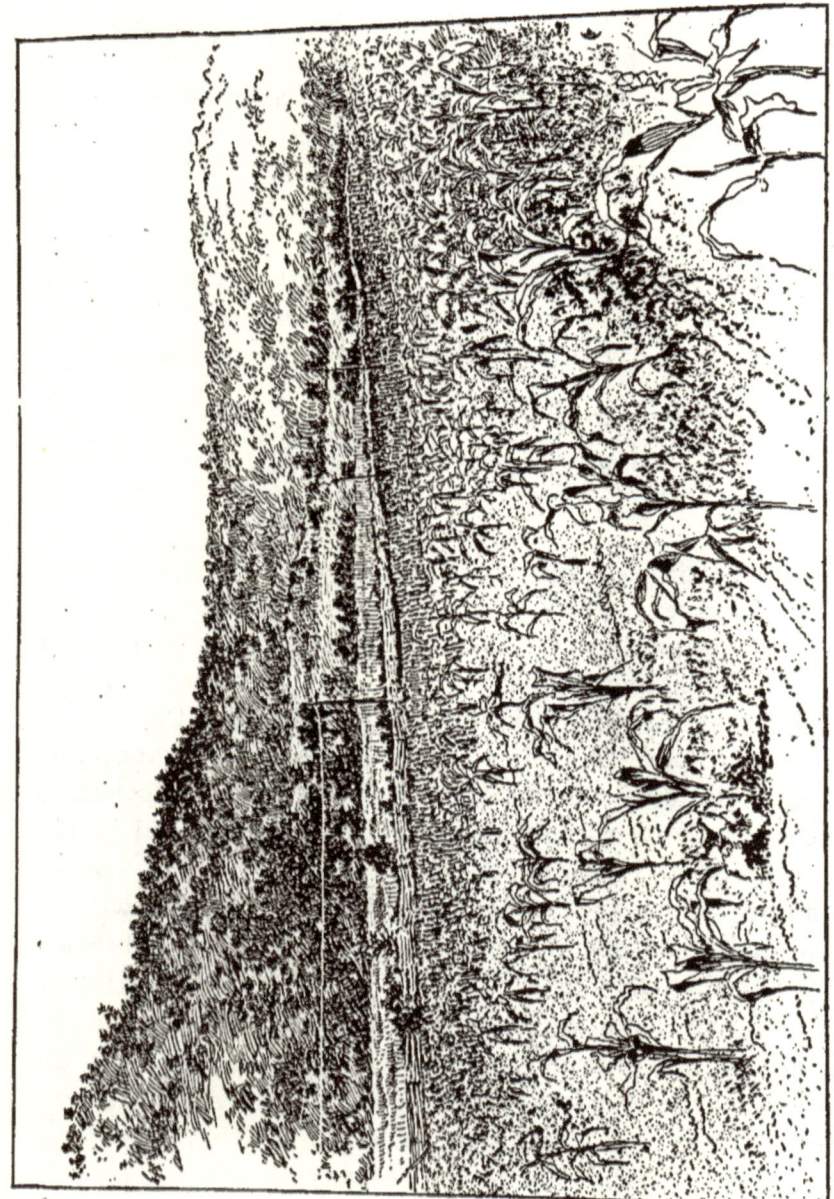

FIG. 7.—Looking Southwest from Lake View Park, Oblique Hotel Site and Forest Parks in Distance.

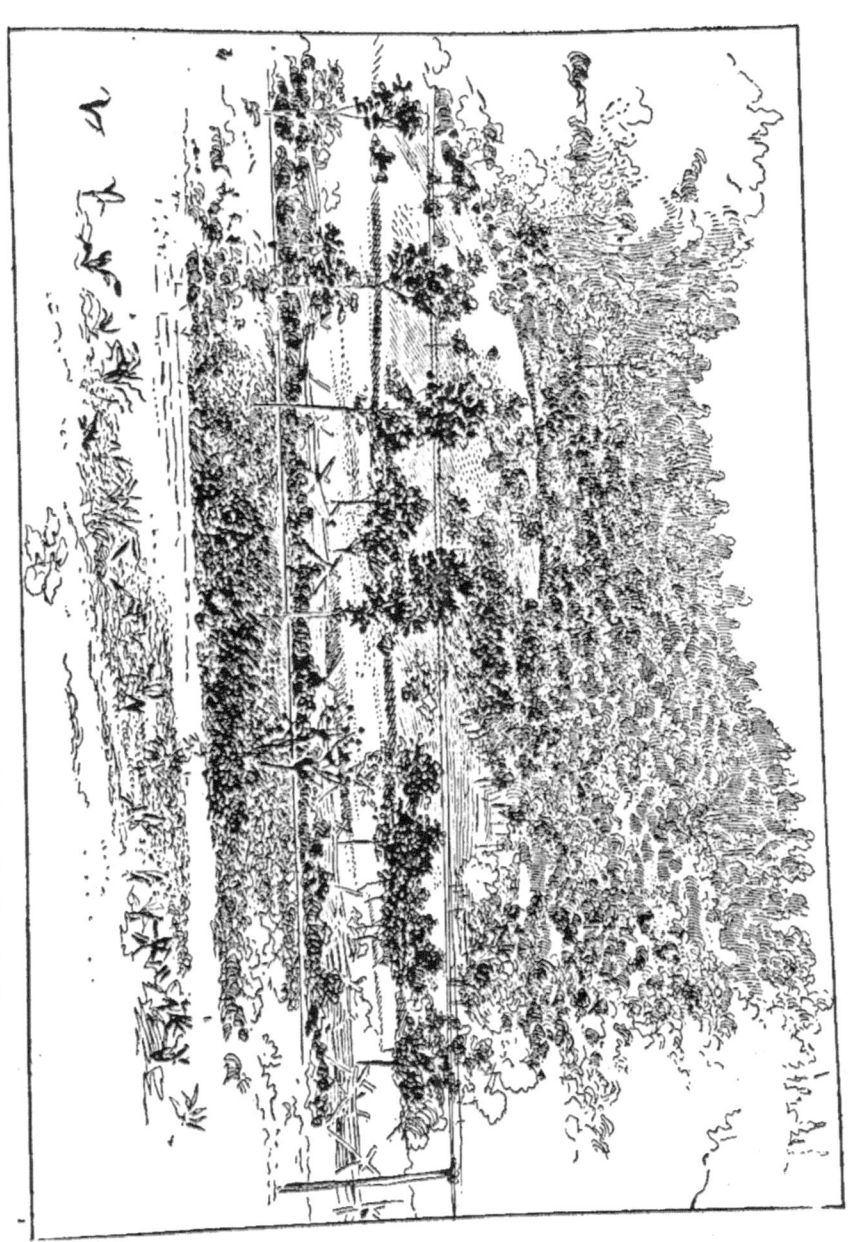

FIG. 8.—Oblique Hotel Site, as seen from French Broad River, Looking South.

matter to convey this delicious water to any residence by means of an aqueduct, with but little cost.

In the rear of the hotel site we can make a fine game park. From the base of the mountain to the apex is 930 feet, at an angle of about 22° (see Fig. 10). Wild grapes grow to perfection on these mountains.

At the base of this mountain will be located a fine stable, and between this and the hotel we have a very desirable piece of ground nicely adapted for a croquet and play ground. In front of the hotel, and about one-quarter down the incline will be a fine tennis park (see map). The front and sides of this beautiful hotel site are on an angle of about 22°, and are so formed as to admit of the most beautiful terraces with but little cost. On each side of the hotel site we have a good number of very desirable elevated sites for private residences (see map and Figs. 11 and 12), with fine mountain parks in background, and the beautiful waters of the mammoth river rolling and sparkling below.

In Fig. 11 we get a fine view looking west, showing the front of a few elevated residence lots.

Looking east we get a splendid view of a part of East Oblique City site (see Fig. 12).

From the hotel site Lake View and the manufacturing sites can be seen, when the timber is cut away and the lake is formed by dam No. 3. This will add much to the attractiveness of our delightful resort, for on Lake View, and Lake Minnehaha, we shall have a fine pleasure yacht and small pleasure boats at an early day.

As we stand on these beautiful mound-like elevations, looking over the old plantation below (which is now covered with cornfields, trees and bushes), in our mind's eye we seem to see in the near future a busy commercial and manufacturing metropolis, with many cozy homes. Before us we see mam-

Fig. 9.—French Broad River and Deer Park Mountains, as seen from Oblique Hotel Site.

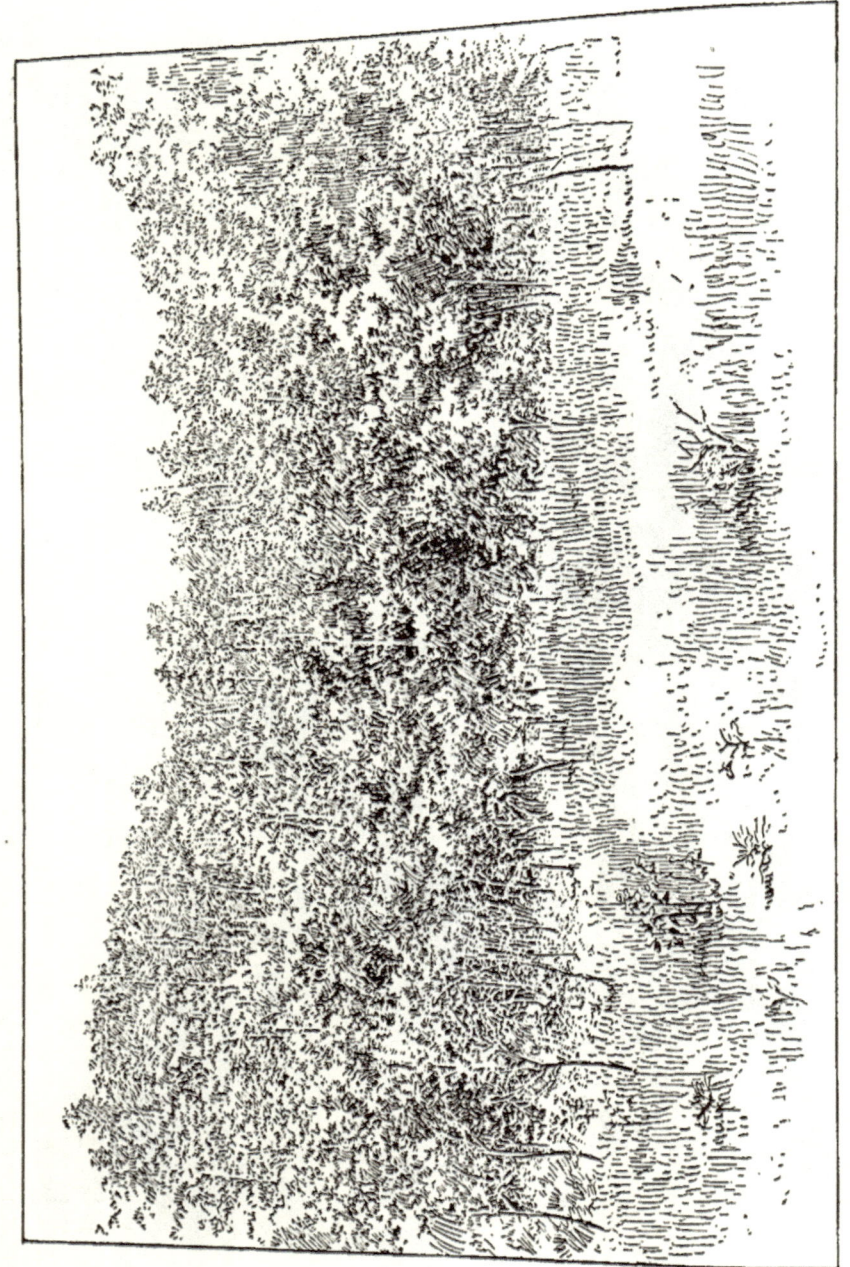

FIG. 10.—Forest Park, in rear of Oblique Hotel Site.

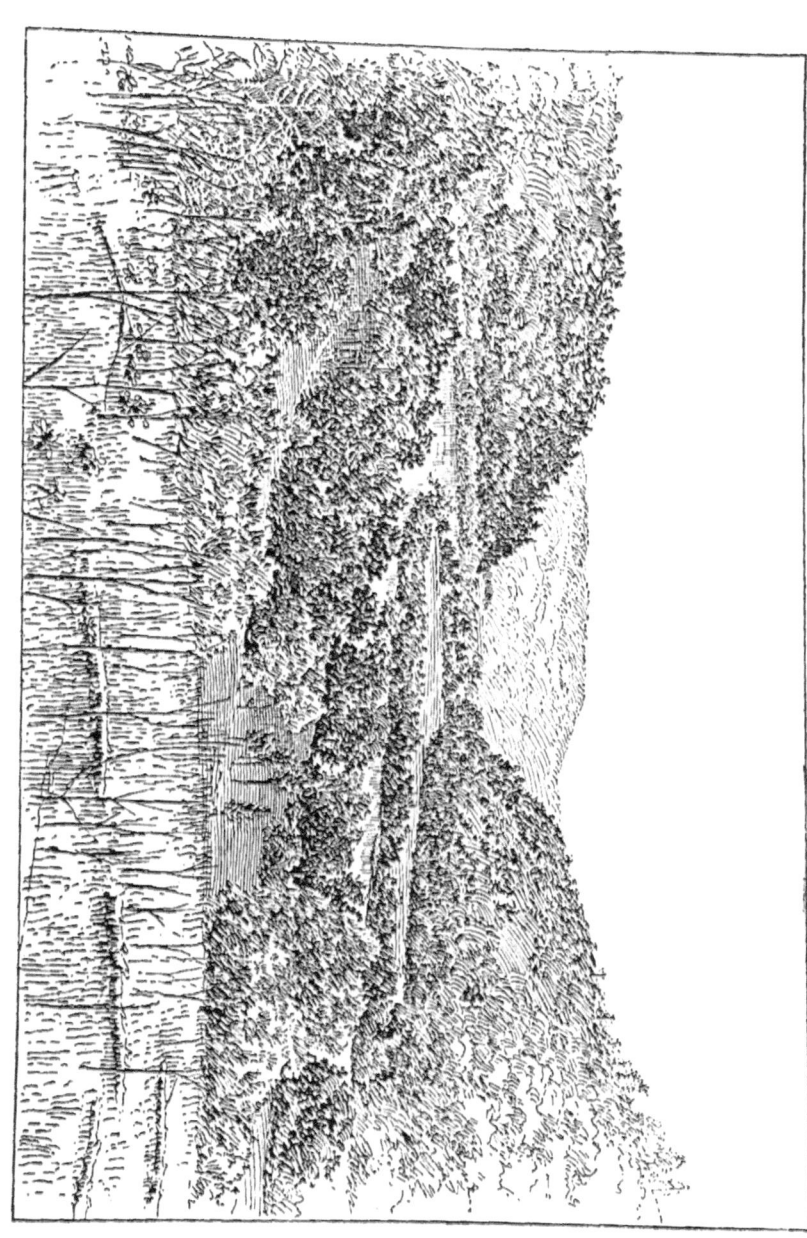

FIG. 11.—Looking down French Broad, from Oblique Hotel Site.

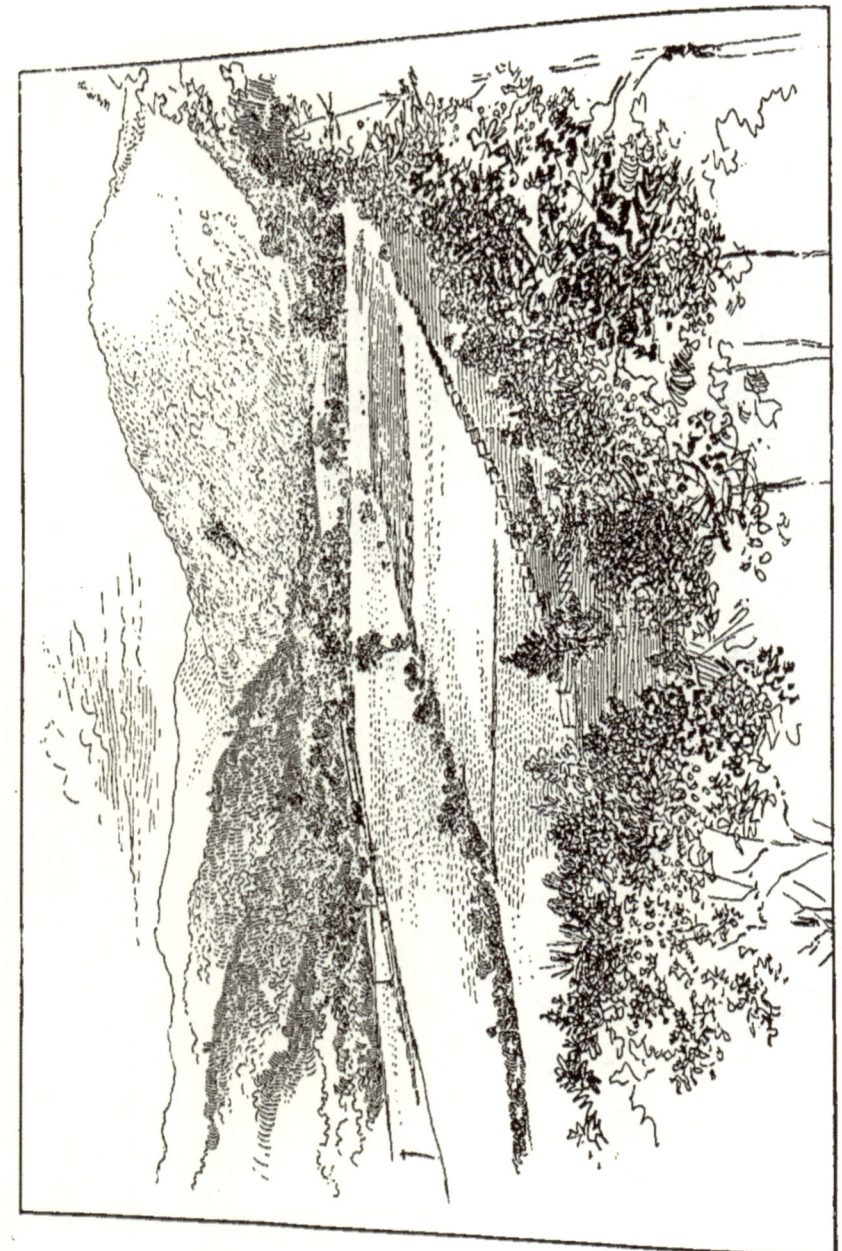

FIG. 12.—Rock House Mountain and Deer Park, as seen from Oblique Hotel Site.

moth manufacturing establishments from which arises the hum of machinery. We seem to see molten metal seething in heavy cauldrons, and anon we see it run like glowing liquid into moulds from which castings in many shapes and forms are taken. We hear the regular and monotonous sound of gigantic power hammers, as they fall regularly with mighty force on the glowing and yielding blocks and bars of highly heated metal, shaping them into the desired forms with as much ease as though they were the most ductile things imaginable.

Now from our day dream in the future let us go back to that which does exist, and with which we are familiar.

Wolf Creek.

AS an all-wise and merciful God has laid out everything in and about our proposed town so much to our liking, let us see what he has done to furnish our temperance city with pure water. Aside from numerous springs, and the sparkling waters of the mighty river, we see he has given us the refreshing and health-giving waters of the limpid Wolf Creek, and from this we can get an ample supply to furnish a large city with pure mountain spring water which can not be excelled in the United States.

This creek takes its rise about 8 miles south of our proposed city, and is fed by numerous mountain springs which rapidly increase its volume, and soon we find it rushing down the mountains, coursing through the valleys, and finally treasured in the mighty French Broad.

He who made the earth and all it contains, and the deep sea and all that is in it, has wisely made a provision for building a large reservoir in which to hold a good supply of this life-giving beverage, which we can depend upon for future use. Go with me a short distance up this beautiful creek, and I will show you a most wonderful formation by which if we build a solid stone dam 60 feet or more in height and about 150 feet across its top, between two gigantic mountains, it will give us an artifical lake about 450 feet across its widest place, and 500 yards long. If we build the dam 75 feet high it will give us an area of water which will be more than twice that size.

This dam will be built of stone and cement; it will be 20 feet wide on the top, and 30 feet at the base. A projection will be so formed on the top as to make a beautiful cascade of the water which will flow over the dam.

On the top of this dam, the entire length, will be erected a fine building, which will constitute a boat-house and Horticultural building, stocked with beautiful flowers and shrubbery. Between this building and the top of the dam will be placed a fine screen to prevent the trout (with which this lake is to be stocked) from escaping. At the upper end of the lake and at ~~Bee~~ Branch screens will also be placed.

A short distance below where the head of this beautiful lake will be (see Fig. 13) we get a fine view of Wolf Creek. Our lovely sheet of water will cover the entire ground seen in Fig. 13, and will flow back nearly up to the Peck residence, and a little above the foot-bridge about 100 feet below the house (see Fig. 14). This reservoir once built we have one of the finest trout lakes in the United States, as Wolf Creek is the natural habitat of the beautiful speckled trout. Usually they are caught here as fast as they are large enough to take bait, consequently do not attain a large size ; but give them protection and plenty of room in such a lake as can be made here, and we will soon have speckled beauties which would tip the scales at three pounds or more. Indeed we would

34

*word crossed out above: original = "Rhea" / written = "Bee"

FIG. 13.—Looking up Wolf Creek, Peck House in Distance.

FIG. 14.—Bridge Across Wolf Creek, at Upper End of Lake Minnehaha, Peck House in Distance.

FIG. 15.—View of Peck Residence, Looking North.

then have a perfect paradise for the disciples of Izaak Walton. Here we will have a lovely lake completely surrounded by gigantic mountains, studded with timber, which preclude the possibility of heavy winds, making one of the most delightful places imaginable for pleasure boating.

> For here 'neath mistletoe and myrtle's lovely green,
> 'Neath azure skies where gentle zephyrs fan the cheek,
> We'd have a lovely, cozy nook, by mortals seldom seen;
> 'T would be a restful haven for weary souls to seek.

The Peck house, of which we have a fine view standing above it looking down the creek (see Fig. 15), was built by Dr. Isham Peck, who was a large, wealthy planter of the State of Louisiana, a gentleman of culture and refinement. Tiring of plantation life and its attendant cares and annoyances, and longing for some place where he could find peaceful rest, where he could study Nature and enjoy her pleasures in quiet retirement, he put his large farming interests in the hands of an agent, and with his family moved to Wolf Creek. Selecting a site in a shaded glen, where the majestic mountains stood around like faithful sentinels to ward off the heat of summer and make the winters seem like a long-continued, delightful autumn, he erected this comfortable house, where he spent in peaceful retirement the remainder of a long life. This delightful home, presided over by the generous, hospitable Doctor and his agreeable and accomplished wife, was made a place of pleasurable associations. Below this, and around our charming lake when it is made, we have a good number of the most delightful residence lots, which will be elevated above the lake, carriage road, and proposed railroad.

A reservoir once formed here, and we have a fine water supply, which can be thrown over the whole town without the expensive process of forcing it from the river by costly

Fig. 16.—Wolf Creek Glen.

machinery; here we see a large saving for the town. We see among the possibilities of the future a railroad running up the mountain along this beautiful creek, as this is the most economical way to get many millions of valuable timber from this section of country. This road can be utilized to run passenger conveyances from town to the top of this range of mountains, a distance of about 9 miles, where one can stand and look into 7 States. This is a grand lookout, as at this point we have an altitude of 4,800 feet above the sea, so given by Government survey, "Uncle Sam" having a signal station here. It is only a matter of time when a building will be erected here to accommodate pleasure seekers.

On our way up Wolf Creek we have a beautiful glen (see Fig. 16) surrounded by a luxuriant growth of splendid foliage and fine timber which towering high above forms a fine screen and gives a mellow light, making one of those enchanting pictures which artists love to paint. Near by we get a fine timber view, which shows about an average of timber in this section (see Fig. 17). Here we find grape vines climbing to the tops of the trees.

Farther up this beautiful creek we have a charming cascade, to which we give the appropriate title of "Minnehaha," as it is indeed "laughing water," as the Indian name implies. This delightful place has such a power of enchantment that a true lover of Nature is always loth to leave it. The beautiful waterfall leaps over a shelving ledge, falling in a fine sheet into a deep pool below, from which arises a halo of spray, which permeates the atmosphere and makes it most agreeable and refreshing (see Fig. 18). This exquisitely lovely spot is well worthy of the artist's brush. It would be close to the railroad, and without much cost could be made a most delightful little nook, which could be fitted out

FIG. 17.—Timber View on Wolf Creek.

FIG. 18.—Minnehaha Cascade on Wolf Creek.

with a cozy pleasure station, where one could stop and re
fresh both body and mind, by drinking "Dame Nature's"
limpid beverage from this sylvan fountain, and studying
the beautiful and mysterious works of an all-wise God.

To go to the top of the mountain and return would be a
delightful and entertaining trip, and in time this would be a
paying investment for its fortunate owners.

Exploration of Timber Accessible to French Broad River and its Tributaries.

WE will next call the reader's attention to the great importance of this splendid water-way as a channel by
which countless millions of valuable timber can be conveyed
from a vast area of timber-land lying accessible to it and its
tributaries. (See map of French Broad and tributaries.)
When we take into account the fact that this mammoth
river is navigable for timber a practical timber-man can
readily understand its great value as a log conveyer to our
proposed city from a vast area of timber-land, the supply
from which is practically inexhaustible. Of this fact I have
fully satisfied myself.

In the fall of 1892 I engaged a man to accompany me, and
together we left Newport, Tenn., September 3, and arrived at
Hot Springs (10 miles above Wolf Creek) in time for dinner.
In the afternoon we explored on the north side of the river,
where we found about an equal amount of pine and hard
growth. About 7 miles from the river we took an easterly
course back, our object being to get a lookout from the top

of a high mountain. After a good bit of climbing we were well rewarded for our labor. Looking across the river a grand sight met our view, for rising from the banks (which were about three miles distant to the south) we saw an immense tract of timber-land with a gradual incline toward the water. Here countless millions of valuable timber are easily accessible to the French Broad River.

Early on the morning of the 4th we started up Spring Creek, a tributary of the French Broad, where we soon came into heavy timber, principally hard wood in great variety.

Taking a southeasterly course we soon arrived at a point about 5 miles from the river in a fine valley, densely covered with heavy timber. Here we found as fine hemlock as I ever saw. The natives call it spruce pine, but it is the hemlock (*Abies Canadensis*), which grows so commonly in North America. From this valley we diverged to the south, our object being to get sufficient elevation to form an idea of the surrounding country. Arriving at the top of a mountain we had a fine view of the valley below and distant mountains, thickly covered with heavy timber. From here we descended to Spring Creek Valley, which from this point runs nearly parallel with the river, and from 5 to 7 miles away. Toward evening we neared the head of Spring Creek, and were quite ready to put up for the night. We were hospitably entertained by a wealthy farmer, who has a good farm cosily tucked away in this beautiful valley. Our host being a man of high moral character we learned much in regard to the value and extent of the timber in this section of country, and also gained much valuable information of the country we afterward traveled over, which materially helped us in our explorations. Here we found fine fruit, vegetables and grain. This rich soil and fine climate is perfectly adapted to fruit, as apples, peaches, and grapes

44

grow to perfection here. We also found delicious black-berries, which grow very large and are most prolific.

On the morning of the 5th we bade our host good-bye and started across the mountains to Pine Creek. En route we passed through a dense growth of heavy hard-wood timber. As we approached Pine Creek we began to see considerable pine. We explored this creek to within a few miles of the river; here pine predominates. We next explored up Pine Creek, and across to Sandy Mush Creek, where we struck the heavy, hard-wood timber again. We travelled up this creek about 5 miles, and then kept east and about parallel with French Broad River to Turkey Creek, up which we went about 7 miles; from there we went to Mills River.

The creeks we passed are all capable of carrying timber from 5 to 10 miles to their outlets, at high water, by clearing them out.

We travelled up Mills River about 10 miles and then diverged in a southeasterly course, keeping about 5 miles from and nearly parallel with French Broad River. For the last 10 miles the timber was principally second growth, of very fine quality. As we approached Davidson's River we found heavy timber of good quality, principally chestnut, oak and poplar. On our journey through these heavily-timbered mountains and valleys, we saw many fine trees which measured from 3 to 5 feet in diameter 3 feet from the ground, and 50 feet and more to the limbs, and thousands of beautiful trees 18 to 30 inches in diameter, which would not seem to be much smaller 60 feet and more to the limbs. In one group we measured four of these mammoth trees 3 feet from the ground, with a tape line. A chestnut was 6½ feet, and three oaks, 5, 5½ and 6 feet in diameter, and a short distance away we put the tape

45

around an ash which measured 12 feet in circumference 3 feet from the ground. One's eyes are apt to magnify when traveling through heavy timber, especially if they wish to tell a "*big story*" when in camp, or at home. My companion was somewhat inclined this way, for as we advanced on this ash, he called my attention, estimating it to be 3 feet in diameter, when we were perhaps 100 yards away. I replied that it was probably 2 feet, and it did not seem much more; but "presto——!" I was surprised when the tape actually proved it to be 4 feet in diameter. Indeed, it was a giant ash, for they do not attain a large size, although we saw some isolated samples larger than this. In this case we were both on the safe side. My friend was frequently inclined to see trees larger than I did; I do not think he meant to exaggerate, but his eyes seemed to possess a magnifying power, as he often seemed to be under the delusion of a mirage. He seemed to have excellent judgment at meal times, as he was an expert judge of the choice parts of a chicken, and had a very high appreciation for pancakes.

After exhausting nearly a day exploring up Davidson's River we found ourselves nearing the head waters of French Broad River. Here we found immense forests of heavy timber. The next day, after a hard tramp of over 30 miles, we found ourselves (with the assistance of a guide) on the apex of Balsam Mountain, above the head-waters of French Broad River, within 18 miles of the line of South Carolina, having traveled nearly across the southwest corner of the State of North Carolina diagonally, and the most of the way through heavy timber. I am fully qualified to say, that in these mountains and valleys we discovered the finest bodies of timber to be found east of the Rockies. I have seen much fine timber from Maine to California, also from Canada nearly to the Gulf of Mexico, and I think it safe to say that the French Broad River and its tributaries command an inexhaustible supply for our proposed manufacturing city.

I am told there are heavy bodies of pine timber on the north side of French Broad which we did not explore.

Standing on the top of Balsam Mountain we had a fine view of beautiful valleys stretching away in the distance, and lofty mountains looming above the horizon many miles away. Here we saw a sight which could not fail to interest a practical lumberman—many thousands of acres of virgin forests of fine timber. At the head of these rivers (we were informed by our guide) is good trout fishing, but as we had no time to make the acquaintance of the speckled beauties, we went home with him, and the next morning started across the mountains and valleys for the Great Smoky Mountains.

We made 50 miles in two days, going across the well-known "Pink Beds," which consist of a rich alluvial bottom land, densely covered with heavy timber. We were informed that George Vanderbilt talks of building an immense dam at the lower end of this valley to form a large trout lake, and also that he contemplates surrounding many thousands of acres in this section with wire fence, to embrace all the land between Mills and Davidson's Rivers, for an immense game park. On our journey up we called to see the mansion he is building a few miles above Asheville, N. C. It is a mammoth structure, and when everything is completed will cost over $10,000,000, so we were told.

From the Pink Beds we crossed over Pisgah Ridge (a high range of mountains). We had a laborious climb, this mountain being heavily timbered near its top. However, we were well repaid for our toil. Standing on this immense water-shed we got a magnificent view of the country beyond, which, with the exception of a few small clearings occupied

47

by farmers, is covered with heavy timber as far as the eye can reach. In the near future thousands of fine farms will be taken in this vast section of country.

The people of the South seem blind to their interests. They seem to lack business stamina. By judicious advertising they could easily turn the tide of emigration South, which would soon begin to develop the great natural resources which now lie dormant in this fine climate. The South is by far the best opening for settlement now available in the United States. Let the tide of emigration once turn to the "Sunny South" and we shall soon see such remarkable strides in its prosperity as will astonish the world.

On the west side of Pisgah Ridge (on Pigeon River) the soil is more inclined to be stony than in the country we passed on the French Broad, yet the farmers get good crops here, cropping many consecutive years without fertilizers, so they told us. From Pisgah Ridge we kept down Pigeon River to Henson's Gap, where a heavy storm came on and we had a never-to-be-forgotten tramp of 25 miles across the mountains in a heavy rain. We arrived late in the afternoon, well drenched, at Pigeon Station. Here we obtained comfortable quarters for the night and the next morning took the train for Asheville, N. C., where we changed for Newport, Tenn., arriving there late in the afternoon of the 17th, tired and foot-sore, as we had traveled over 200 miles on foot since we left Hot Springs, N. C., on the morning of the 3d.

My object in making this exploration was principally to satisfy myself as to the amount of timber we could command at Wolf Creek by the French Broad River and its tributaries. I am highly gratified to state that the available supply is practically inexhaustible, for in the vast timbered country we explored there is enough to build and maintain a large manufacturing town for many generations

48

to come. The three greatest factors that go to create and maintain large towns are manufacturing, mining and agricultural resources. Here we find all of these. There is an inexhaustible supply of the very finest timber in great variety in this great timbered region on which we can depend, and it is well-known that the precious metals do exist in paying quantities in the Great Smoky Mountains. Prospecting is in its infancy in this section of the country. The baser metals are plentifully distributed here, as different grades of iron ore crop out in some localities. We also found here black and gray slate of good quality, fine granite, kaolin (the finest china clay), a fine grade of clay for bricks, and an inexhaustible supply of the finest quality of limestone. There is a lasting and fertile soil, capable of producing as fine cereals and vegetables as can be grown east of the Rocky Mountains. Tobacco grows here to perfection; I saw as fine fields of tobacco in the country we explored as in the best tobacco producing section of Kentucky. In confirmation of this, I will quote from the *Harriman Weekly Advance* of February 2, 1893, in which the editor of the *Advance* says:

"Capt. R. H. Bowie, representing the Tennessee and Georgia Association of Chattanooga, is in the city, and met a number of gentlemen at the Board of Trade rooms this morning and made them a short and interesting talk in regard to the plans of the Association he represented, the advantages of tobacco culture, and made the suggestion that the way was open for Harriman to become the market for a large scope of country where the cultivation of the famous weed was entered into by the farmers. He described the 'Bright Tobacco Belt' as being a narrow strip of country extending from West Virginia through southwest Virginia, west· North Carolina, east Tennessee, north Georgia and north Alabama, a distance of about 600 miles, and from 150 to 200 miles in breadth, and the only region where the bright, or yellow, tobacco can be successfully raised. Capt. Bowie said we had much better soil here for tobacco than in Green and Sullivan Counties, where the crop has brought wealth and population into the country, and made lands that five years ago were not worth $5 an acre worth from $25 to $30. Poor soils, that in wheat or corn could hardly pay for the seed planted, would yield fine tobacco and return the grower $75 to $100 per acre.''

I will include east Kentucky in Captain Bowie's "Bright Tobacco Belt." By consulting the map we find that our proposed city is located in the centre of this rich tobacco producing-section of the "Sunny South," which gives us the great advantage of a central market, and will in the near future call for a tobacco factory. It can also be seen that we are in the very heart of this fine fruit-growing section, thus giving us the promise of a mammoth fruit canning establishment before very long.

I will again quote from the *Advance* of same date, in which it says: "Confidence in the future of the South and of this particular place in it, will inspire wonders. And why not confidence? The mineral wealth of this region is undoubted. The marvelous growth of Harriman is abundant proof. The conditions of climate and soil guarantee agricultural developments round about. The possibilities here are boundless."

It will be seen the *Advance* fully confirms what I have said of this remarkable section of country and its future possibilities. 'Tis easy to predict our future prosperity, situated as we are in the very center of this rich agricultural section of the "Sunny South," more particularly when we take into consideration our immense water-power and fine location, which is the key to extensive virgin forests of the finest timber in the country. Then we have (taking everything pertaining to fruit-raising into consideration) one of the most desirable fruit-growing sections in the United States. In the mountains the soil is a strong, rich loam, and in the valleys a deep alluvial, and both of these grow fruit very rapidly. Apple and peach trees come to bearing here much earlier than in the New England States, and quite as early as in California and Oregon. In the mountains apples and grapes grow to perfection and are very prolific. I never saw finer or more healthy apple trees than grow here. Grape vines climb to the tops of the trees and were loaded down with fruit when I saw them. I have eaten fine apples here in the mountains in May, of a delicious flavor and as crisp as we find the best varieties in March in New England. On the subject of fruit-raising, I consider myself competent to judge, as I have had fifteen years' experience as a successful fruit raiser in cold New England, and could prune and graft both apples and small fruits quite as successfully as any of my neighbors. When I speak of fruit culture and preservation, I speak from *much experience*, and *do not borrow my ideas from others, but give facts as they exist*, and the farmers of this section will fully corroborate my statement on this subject. These mountains are the natural home of the apple and grape, as we have an intermediate climate between the two extremes of North and South, with the proper altitude to grow and preserve them to perfection. An experienced fruit farmer fully understands the importance of a cool, dry atmosphere to keep apples in fall and winter. Apples are preserved most perfectly when kept *as cool and dry as possible* (so as not to chill) near the freezing point. In an average winter apples keep in fine condition in a room above ground in this delightful climate. No finer flavored apples can be raised in the United States than are grown in these mountains.

When we take into consideration all of the great natural

advantages and resources which surround Wolf Creek I am fully qualified to say that its equal can not be found in the United States (lying on a railroad, undeveloped); and with as good water-power.

⌧

Recapitulation.

IN addition to explanations already given, let me again give a brief summary of a few of the leading features which make our proposed city a place chosen by Nature as a health and pleasure resort, as well as a wealthy manufacturing metropolis. After investigating carefully, and satisfying myself fully by exploring the extensive and valuable timber and mineral lands accessible to Wolf Creek and the French Broad River and its tributaries, I purchased the two plantations which constituted our town-site. Having secured this splendid water-power I got what had cost me much valuable time in looking for, and which exceeded my most sanguine expectations, as I saw a grand opportunity to establish a manufacturing plant that, by judicious management, would form a nucleus around which other manufacturers would locate, and in time make a great manufacturing city. The pleasant and healthful attractions of this neighborhood, which have already been highly appreciated by many thousands, would at the same time be highly remunerative as a health and pleasure resort. It has the finest, most healthful and most equable climate in the United States, being a medium between North and South. The summers at Wolf Creek give a mean temperature of about 70° Fahrenheit, and the winters about 40°. Its lowest temperature in winter very

52

rarely reaches zero, while its maximum heat in summer is frequently far below that of Boston, Montreal, Chicago or St. Paul.

The elevation at Wolf Creek is about 1,600 feet above the sea, while that of the Great Smoky Mountains, about 8 miles south of Wolf Creek, is 4,800 feet. From the latter point a view can be had of parts of seven States. We have as good water as can be found in the United States, being from pure free-stone springs. Our fine chalybeate and sulphur springs are highly beneficial to invalids, as many can testify. Our nights are delightfully cool throughout the summer season, when one can sleep comfortably under blankets. We are not troubled with mosquitoes, which are so annoying in low lands and marshy places during the warm weather. On the whole, our location is unsurpassed by any place in the South, being free from malaria, consumption, catarrhal and bronchial troubles, and possessing, as it does, an equable temperature and a pure and bracing atmosphere. Invalids afflicted with those diseases soon find relief here. The climate is similar to that of the Rogue River Valley of Southern Oregon, near the north line of California. We have many advantages here which are wanting there, however.

There are the different soils, which are well adapted to fruit, vegetables, tobacco, corn and wheat. I have seen as fine wheat growing here as I saw in the far-famed Willamette and Sacramento valleys of Oregon and California. Our close proximity to the cotton fields of the Carolinas assures us of one of the largest cotton-manufacturing cities in the United States, not excepting the great cotton factories of Maine. They have to ship the raw material from the South at great expense, while we have it at our very doors.

Our immense water-power, cheap labor, and short haul to the seaboard assure us of large woolen factories in the near

53

future, as here we have climate and soil exactly adapted to sheep-raising. The fine wool merinos (to which the long, cold winters of the North proved so disastrous) winter here in perfect condition.

Taking everything into consideration, we have in prospect one of the largest manufacturing cities in the South, possessing a most valuable water-power, railroad connections, and the best location, as yet undeveloped, to be found in the United States. All other available water-powers have been taken up within the last few years.

We shall soon profit by our fortunate investment in securing this valuable manufacturing location, as Northern manufacturers are fast beginning to locate their plants in the "Sunny South." In proof of this I will quote a few of many reports which the Knoxville *Journal* of June 29 reprints from the Chattanooga *Tradesman*. It says:

"The *Tradesman* has compiled a report of the new industries established in the Southern States during the three months ending June 30, which shows a total of 659 against 779 and 673 for the corresponding periods in 1892 and 1891 respectively."

After reporting many industries which have lately started in the South, the *Tradesman* says:

"There was a spurt in canning factories, showing that the South is beginning to utilize the surplus fruits and vegetables. Thirty-seven were established in three months, against twenty-nine and seventeen in the corresponding periods of the preceding years: Georgia leading with ten, Texas following with five, Mississippi and Tennessee four each, Alabama and South Carolina three each, Florida and Virginia each two. The development of the textile industry shows no sign of abatement. Seventy-two cotton and woolen mills were organized during the quarter, against fifty-nine and thirty-four in the corresponding periods of

54

1892 and 1891. North Carolina leads with nineteen, South Carolina following with fourteen, Alabama nine, Georgia ten, Texas and Virginia each seven, and Mississippi three. Forty-two flour mills were established : Tennessee leading with ten, North Carolina having nine, Virginia six, Kentucky five, Florida and Texas each three. Forty-three mining and quarrying companies were established, West Virginia leading with fourteen, and Texas and Tennessee each having seven.''

The above report shows that our nearest neighbor, North Carolina, leads with nineteen cotton and woolen mills. She also comes next to us in flour mills.

When I called the attention of the leading members of our company to this remarkable location and my intention to combine it with my valuable invention and form a company, they were at once interested, and after looking over our proposed site, quickly decided to join me. We organized immediately, and I secured the assistance of one of the best civil engineers in the South, Major R. C. McCalla, of Tuscaloosa, Alabama, who has carefully surveyed and laid out the town site, made estimates of lots, etc.

Major McCalla's Report.

OBLIQUE CITY LOT GROUND.

CAPACITY of ground for lots from Wolf Creek to the cattle guard on George Allen's upper line is 160 business lots, 111 residence lots, and 17 very valuable, highly-elevated residence lots.

Capacity of ground for lots from Wolf Creek to Rhea Branch is 336 residence lots, and 30 elevated residence lots

100 x 200 feet, between the Allen reservation and Rhea Branch.

Capacity of ground for lots from Rhea Branch to Buffalo Rock is 60 residence lots, and 40 elevated residence lots, 100 feet front by 200 feet deep.

Capacity of ground for lots from dam No. 3 to upper end of bottom is 160 residence lots.

Capacity of ground for lots on George Allen's place, the bottom between the railroad and river, will furnish 192 residence lots, and 320 elevated residence lots south of the railroad.

Capacity of ground for lots around Minnehaha Lake is 31 elevated residence lots, 100 feet front by 200 feet deep.

Condensed Statement Made from the Above Details.

859 residence lots, counting five persons to each lot, will
accommodate . . . . 4,295 persons
421 residence lots, counting five persons to each lot, will
accommodate . . . . 2,105 "
17 large, elevated residence lots will accommodate . . . 170 "
_____
Estimated ground-floor population . . . . . . 6,570 "

R. C. McCALLA,
Civil Engineer.

Wolf Creek, Tenn., June 15, 1893.

It will be seen by Major McCalla's report that he only allows one family to each lot. Persons can figure for themselves. In all large cities we find a number of families in a house. We do not propose to use any misleading or coloring matter, but to let every one make his own calculations. Were we to cut up our large, elevated residence sites into lots 50 x 125 it can be seen it would add largely to the number we now have. These fine, elevated residence lots will be worth

56

more to our company than if they were divided up and sold in small ones, as they are adapted to those who wish to build a fine house, with plenty of room for lawns and parks.

As to the worth of our investment, our valuable patent is richly worth the major part of our capitalization. Its importance is already acknowledged by the best mechanics here and in Europe. It is invaluable, and we certainly have the monopoly in the great United States. To show the high estimate in which our patent and site are held where their value is known, I have already consummated a deal for several lots of valuable timber and mineral lands in which I have paid one-half in stock in our company at par, and am negotiating with other parties for lands on the same terms. Were our lots to sell at such prices, and in proportion to their value, as lots brought in Harriman, Tenn., at the first auction sale there, before any improvements were made (which was $604,000 for 574 lots), we should realize a handsome margin above our entire capitalization of $1,500,000. I am told lots were sold at the first auction sale in Middlesborough as high as $490 per front foot. There they have no water power, and the town lies in a depression, and in heavy storms much of it is flooded, while our proposed site is well out of reach of the highest floods.

Then we have a valuable patent and two new machines for which I have applied for patents, to which I give our company a right in the United States, which, when in operation, will reduce the cost of manufacture to a minimum. These machines, being *entirely new*, are a solid monopoly in the United States, as well as in Canada and Europe. Our work made from timber cut by our new process has only to be seen to be appreciated. Wherever beauty of wood is called for it is invaluable, and the great number

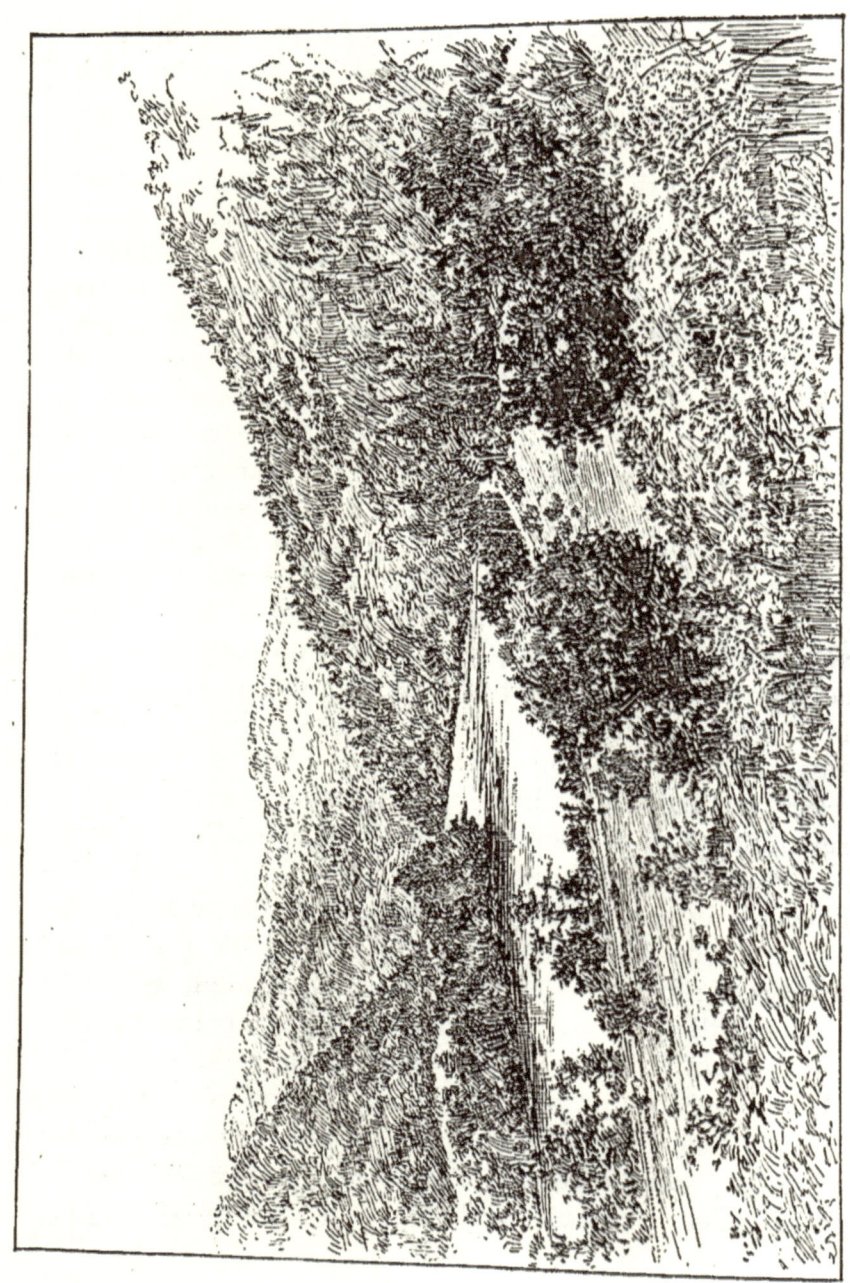

FIG. 19.—View up French Broad River, from Elevated Resident Lot, Mountain Glen, Rock House Cave to Right.

of different designs for which it is so perfectly adapted is but faintly understood by those who first see it. Wherever panels of any description are called for it is indispensable. It is adapted for various uses in fine furniture of all kinds, also wainscoting, ceiling, tiling for the most beautiful floors, and for finishing in passenger coaches, street cars, vessel cabins, banks, churches, and all kinds of buildings where beauty of wood is called for. For musical instruments, the undertaking business, fancy doors and blinds, and for other purposes too numerous to mention it is very valuable. By this process we get beautiful panels of all descriptions from small and unmerchantable timber, thus leaving us a large margin of profit, more particularly from the crude material. We can ship these panels sawed, kiln-dried and planed to various points in the United States, and also to all European countries when once our dam is built and mills in operation, the capacity of which will enable us to fill large demands at home and abroad. We shall first utilize the power furnished by dam No. 3. Here we get an 11-foot dam and a 1-foot blind race, which gives us a 12-foot fall. Our flume will be 60 feet wide and 1,300 feet long. Side-walls of flume will be built of stone, top and bottom of wood. Side-walls will form a solid foundation for twenty or more mills and factories, depending upon the amount of power each will utilize. Our mill and factory combined will occupy the first section of the flume and will be 300 feet long and three stories high. This will leave us 1,000 feet of flume, which we propose to sell and give away to manufacturers who want the space. Building sites, with yard room and power, will be given to seven manufacturers, to whom we will give a warranty deed without any restrictions excepting that they will be bound to work a certain number of hands at least 10 months in each year for 5 consecutive years. The number

FIG. 20.—Fishing on French Broad, Rock House Mountain in Distance.

of hands to which each factory will be required to give steady employment will depend upon capacity of factory, amount of power used and kind of business carried on.

We do not propose to do what too many " Boom Towns " have done, which is to give power and site for a term of only 10 or 20 years, after which the recipient will find himself at the mercy of the company who own the water-right, and be obliged to submit to an annual tax which will prove very onerous, and this too after he has gotten his mills in operation and can not leave them without a great sacrifice. Remember, this perpetual and absolutely free power and site is guaranteed to seven manufacturers who take the seven manufacturing lots we *give away* (see contract of agreement, page 86).

Our Object in Giving Away

SEVEN lots to manufacturers is to bring workmen with their families, who *must have steady employment*, and by this means give our town an *honest and healthy start.* We cordially invite all honest and worthy people who may be engaged in any branch of legitimate industry to come and build their mills and factories in our *moral and temperance city.* We want it distinctly understood that we have no room or place for *lazy loafers* or *vagrant tramps.* To men of means, who are able to live without work, we give a hearty invitation to come and build their homes in our delightful valley city, which lies nestled down in the midst of the grand old mountains, which form a safe barrier from tempestous storms and *most surely* preclude the possibility of cyclones and blizzards. To all such we offer a hearty welcome and

FIG. 21.—View in Deer Park Glen.

FIG. 22.—Looking up French Broad, from Bluff Across the River Opposite Oblique Hotel Site.

promise to make life as enjoyable, pleasant, and entertaining as possible. To those who are seeking a place of delightful and healthful retirement, where they can build their homes and live a life of ease and comfort, we hold out many inducements. We have a large number of very desirable elevated residence sites with fine forest parks in background. A number of the most desirable of these can have a beautiful lawn in front with a gentle incline toward the lovely French Broad River. From these lawns rise beautiful, mound-like elevations, regularly formed. Between these valuable lots delightful dales descend, each having a limpid brook which, taking its rise at the base of the mountain, meanders down these valleys to the river below.

At Rhea Branch we have a very desirable elevated residence lot (see Fig. 19), containing 23 acres, with an elevation of about 50 feet above the river on the mound where buildings will stand, which is now covered with trees. This lot has a fine chalybeate spring on its west side, and on its east is Rhea Branch and Rock House Mountain. From this point we get a fine view of railroad and river, with a beautiful lawn in front. The picture was taken looking up the river, and consequently does not show the scene we have looking down the river, but is about as represented in Fig. 20.

From Mountain Glen lot we get a fine view of the river and mountain scenery below the point illustrated in Fig. 20. This picture was taken just above the junction of Wolf Creek and the river. Below this is a delightful glen (see Fig. 21). From the Bluff just below this glen we get a splendid view up the river (see Fig. 22), also a view down the river, showing elevated residence lots near lower point of the mountain on opposite side of the river, below Oblique Hotel site (see Fig. 23). Looking across the river we see a part of Oblique Hotel site and elevated residence lots west of it. Lot No. 1

FIG. 23.—Looking down French Broad, from Bluff Opposite Oblique Hotel Site.

Fig. 24.—Oblique Hotel Site, and Elevated Residence Lots, as seen from Bluff Across River.

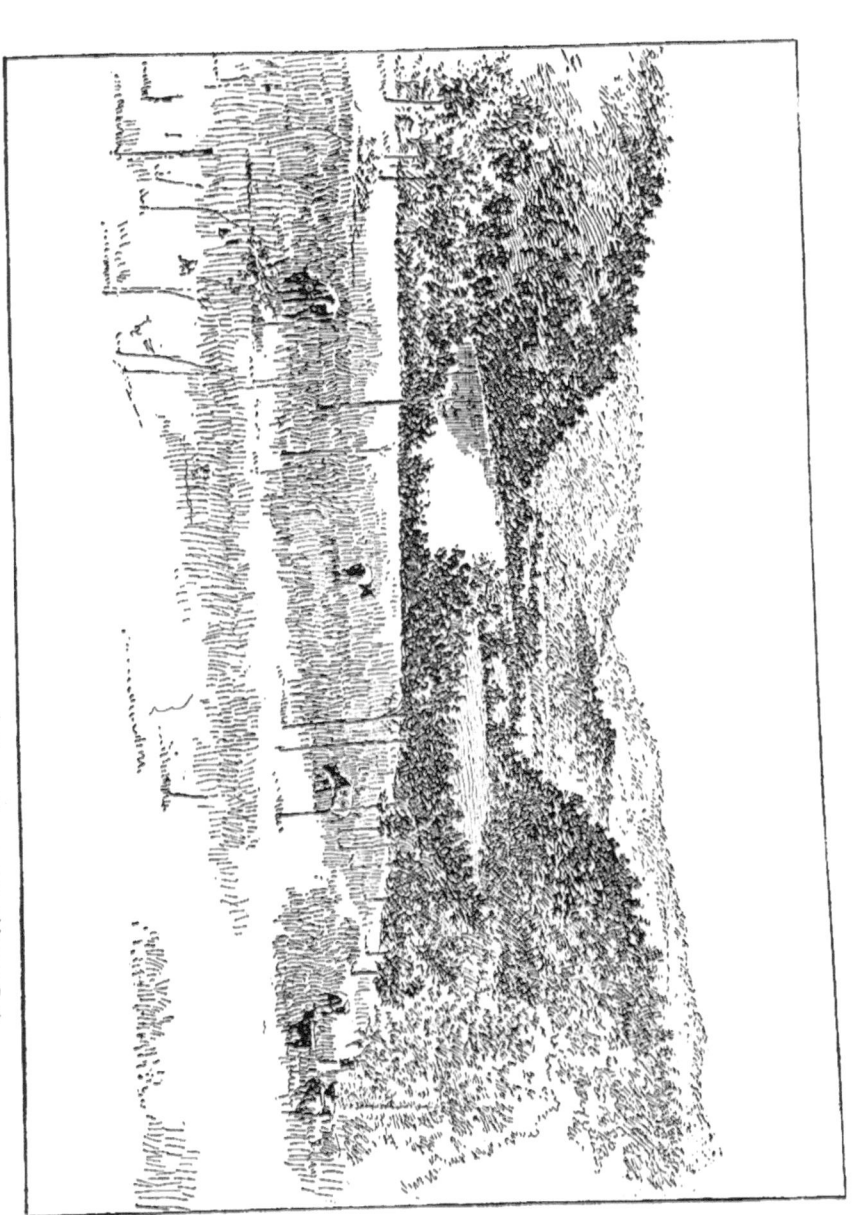

FIG. 25.—Looking down French Broad, from West, No. 1 Elevated Residence Lot.

FIG. 26.—Looking North from Elevated Residence Lot No. 1, West of Oblique Hotel Site.

is seen quite plainly, but other fine lots west of No. 1 do not show clearly in this view, as they are partly covered with fine second-growth timber (see Fig. 24).

East of hotel site we have two beautiful elevated residence lots. These lovely mounds are thickly covered with fine timber, of which the purchaser may preserve as much as he wishes, cutting down the remainder. Most of the other elevated lots have the same advantage. The view from these lots (when the timber is cut and superfluous limbs pruned off) will be the same as seen in Fig. 12. A part of the timber on them can be seen to the right in Fig. 12, and a part of the lawns are also seen, fronting on Jackson Avenue (see map).

East elevated residence lot No. 1 has $6\frac{2}{3}$ acres from lawn to base of mountain; from base of mountain to top, $6\frac{1}{4}$ acres of forest park.

East elevated lot No. 2 has $8\frac{3}{4}$ acres from lawn to base of mountain; from base of mountain to top, $8\frac{3}{4}$ acres of forest park.

From west elevated residence lot No. 1 we get a grand view looking down the river (see Fig. 25). From here can be seen a part of West Oblique City, south of river. Dam No. 4 will be located opposite the point of the mountain shown to the right, where a small view of the river can be seen in Fig. 25. This lot has $6\frac{1}{4}$ acres from railroad to base of mountain; from base of mountain to top $6\frac{3}{4}$ acres of forest park. From this point we get a splendid view across the river (see Fig. 26). This is a very desirable lot, having a fine chalybeate spring on its west side, near where residence would stand. There is a beautiful forest park in background (see Fig. 27).

West elevated residence lot No. 2 is mostly covered with trees. This fine site, like those adjoining, is high above the

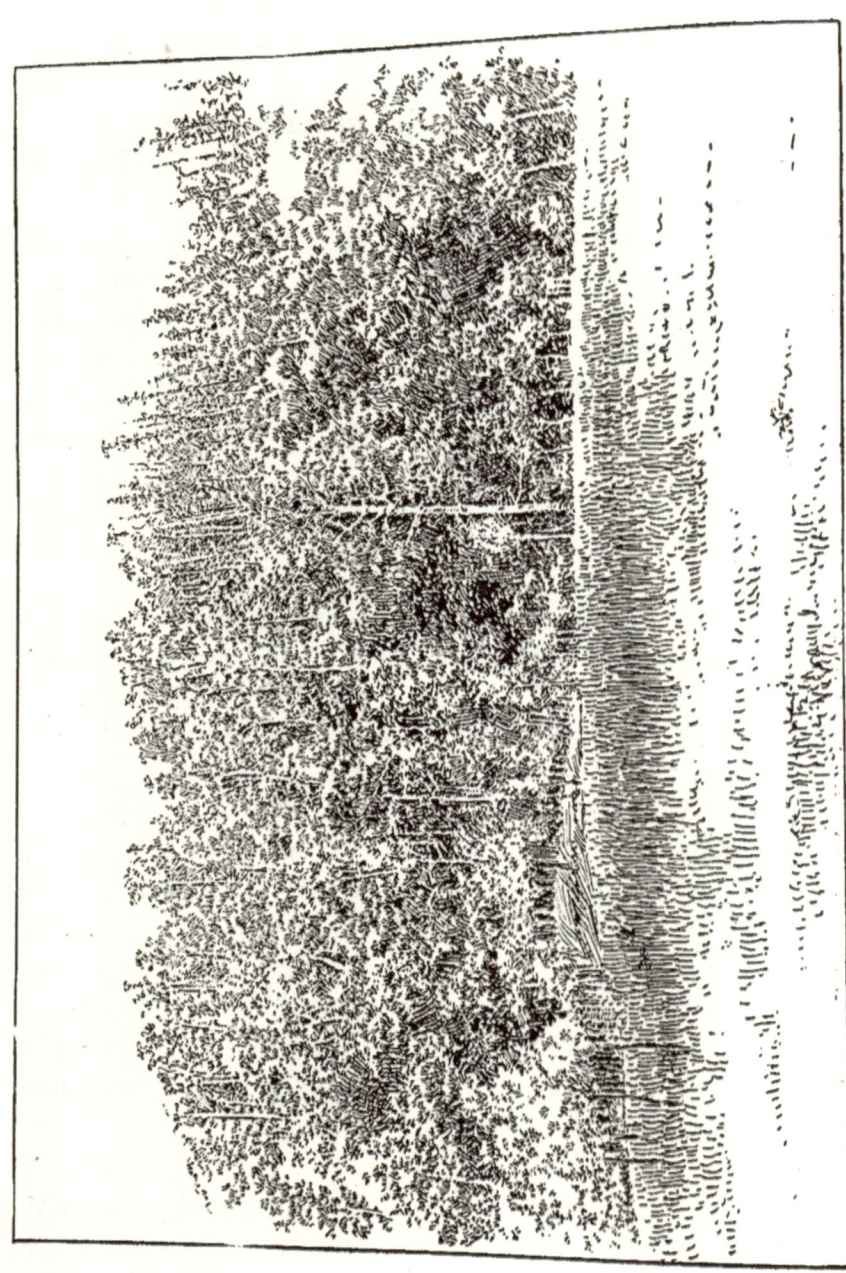

FIG. 27.—Looking South from No. 1 Elevated Residence Lot, Showing Mountain Park in Background.

river, about 75 feet, and contains $5\frac{1}{4}$ acres from railroad to base of mountain ; from base of mountain to top, $3\frac{2}{3}$ acres.

Elevated residence lot No. 3 contains 11 acres from railroad to base of mountain ; from base to top $8\frac{7}{10}$ acres. This valuable tract is mostly covered with timber, which prevented us from getting a good view of mountains in rear, but we got one from in front near the river (see Fig. 28).

West elevated residence lot No. 4 contains 10 acres from railroad to base of mountain ; from base to top $12\frac{4}{10}$ acres forest park.

West elevated residence lot No. 5 contains 15 acres from railroad to base of mountain ; from base to top $11\frac{1}{2}$ acres forest park..

West elevated residence lot No. 6 contains $3\frac{1}{2}$ acres from railroad to base of mountain ; from base to top 3 acres forest park.

West elevated residence lot No. 7 contains 19 acres from railroad to top of mountain ; about 7 acres of this is forest park.

West elevated residence lot No. 8 contains $9\frac{1}{10}$ acres from railroad to top of mountain ; about one-half of this is forest park.

West elevated residence lot No. 9 contains $8\frac{4}{5}$ acres from railroad to top of mountain ; about two-thirds of this is forest park.

Between elevated residence lot No. 9 and point of mountain we have at least 6 fine elevated residence lots, giving a fine view of railroad, bottom lands and river, with beautiful mountain scenery across the river. These lots are directly in front of the large lake to be formed by dam No. 4, with a high elevation above it. This lake, which we call Lake Lomond, after the queen of Scottish lakes, will be nearly one mile long, with an area of over 40 acres. A fine view can be had of a part of East and West Oblique City standing near where this dam will be (see Figs. 29 and 30). A part of the hotel site and lots Nos. 1, 2 and 3 can be seen in this cut, with Observatory Mountain in the distance.

Looking down the river from dam No. 4, we get a fine view of a part of West Oblique City and valley below dam, with the beautiful Chestnut Mountain to the left (see Fig. 30).

Standing on the elevated plateau we get a splendid view of a part of the west town, and of the beautiful scenery in the distance (see Fig. 31). We also get a fine view across the French Broad which shows nearly up to dam No. 4, and a part of the valley (see Fig. 32).

From many of the elevated residence lots in the west town we get splendid birds-eye views of the beautiful lake which is to be formed by dam No. 4.

Temperance and Labor.

FROM our by-laws (contained in this Prospectus) it can be seen that the liquor traffic and immoral practices are strictly prohibited in title deeds. Consequently, saloons and immoral resorts will never be allowed, with their inevitable degrading and destructive influences on labor and its products. Where sobriety and thrift reign supreme, we find comfortable and happy homes, and where saloons with their baleful influences abound we find crime, depravity, and woe. It is a well-established economic fact that sober labor, free from saloons, yields a good percentage of gain to its employers over labor where intoxicants are allowed. Every manufacturer who has been troubled with dissipated em-

FIG. 28.—Looking North from Elevated Residence Lot No. 3.

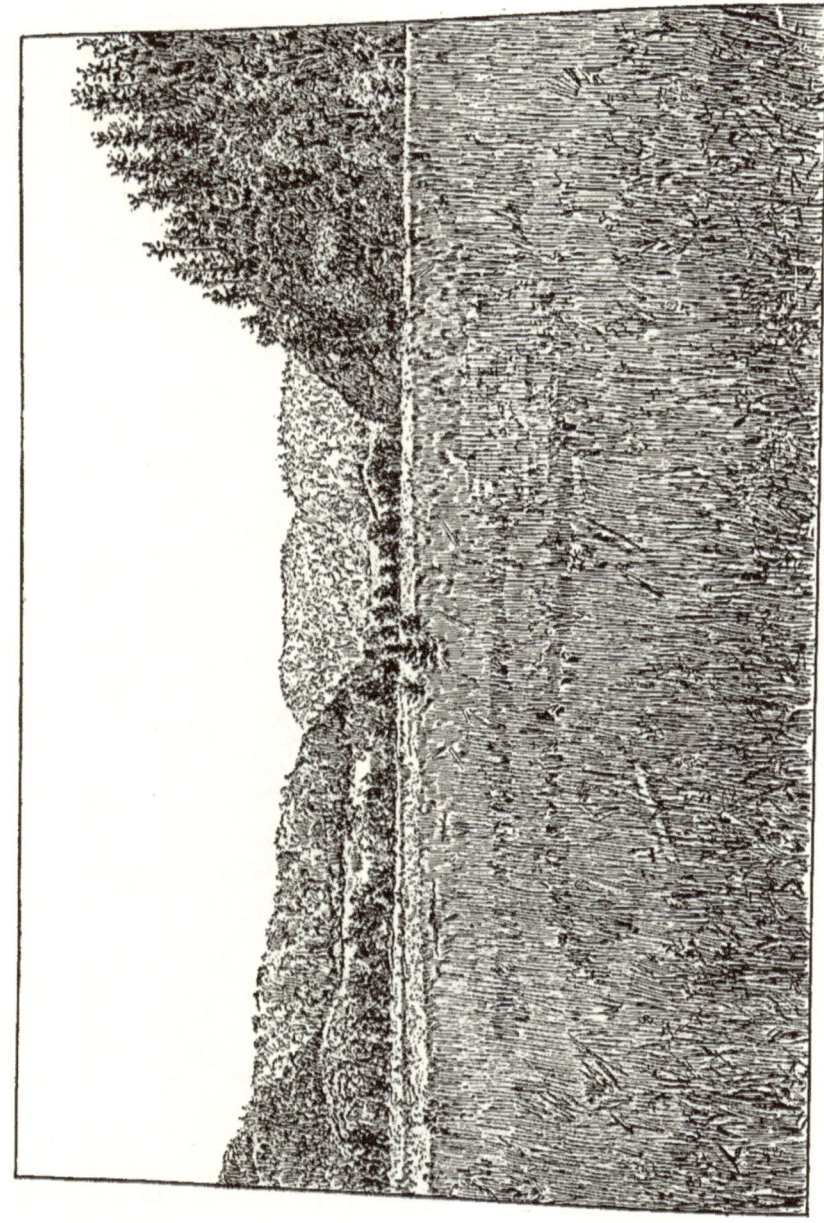

Fig. 29.—Looking up French Broad Valley from West Oblique City Site, Showing Hotel Site, and Elevated Residence Lots to the Right.

ployés can corroborate this fact, and large manufacturing plants have yielded much greater dividends in years when the liquor traffic was forbidden and abolished, than in other years when it was permitted. No workmen are so profitable to their employers as those who are strictly temperate in all things, and by reason of their sobriety and industry come into possession of their own homes, strive after superiority, and seek that mutual welfare and good fellowship which is the safe and sure offspring of a temperate and moral life.

❧❀❧

Profitable Investment.

WE propose to employ temperate workmen only, and with our valuable and cheap raw material and improved machinery the cost of the product of our manufactory will be reduced to a minimum. The same rule will apply to all classes of manufacturers who secure a location at Wolf Creek. Our abundant water power will save them a large fraction of cost over steam, dispensing with fireman and engineer, and making a good reduction in insurance rates. It also does away with all risk of explosions.

Under the practical business management secured by the methods which we have outlined, the profits from our manufacturing plant, and also from the sale of lots, are sure to be much better than they can average elsewhere, and by reason of the guarantee made to stockholders, in our Contract of Agreement (which is contained in this Prospectus), it is certain that the stock of the American Oblique Manufacturing and City Development Company will pay good dividends at an early day.

It is also certain, from the conditions referred to, that our

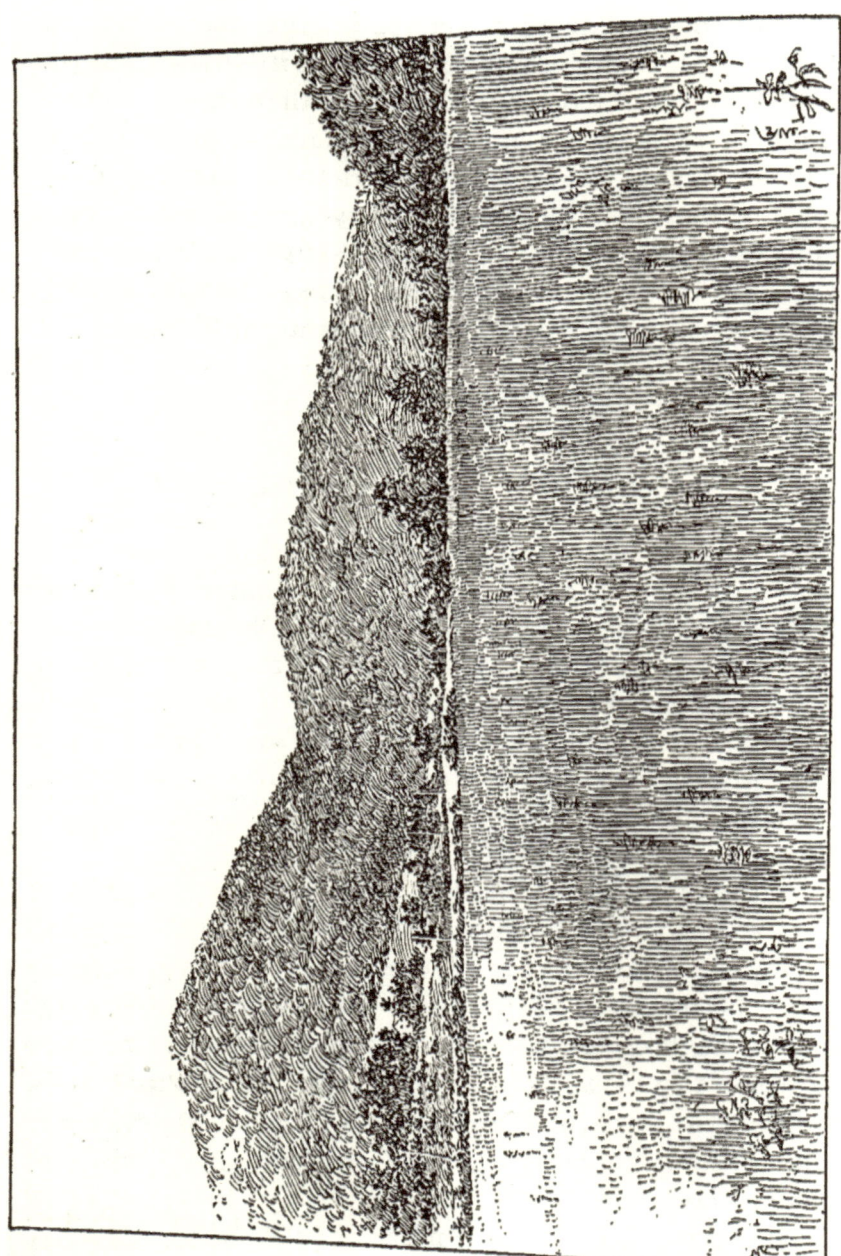

FIG. 30.—Chestnut Mountain, as seen from French Broad Valley. Standing near Dam No. 4.

FIG. 31.—Looking down French Broad from West Oblique City Plateau.

stock will constantly grow in its dividend-paying capacity, which assures all who invest in it that their investment will steadily and surely increase in value; for unless I establish a *twenty-five per cent. annual dividend* from the manufacture and sale of panels, within five years from the commencement of our manufacture, I forfeit my entire interest in our Company. (See Contract of Agreement.) The Company is bound to become one of the most extensive and profitable industrial enterprises which can be found in the South. Since its formation much stock has already *been taken up*, which is good proof of great confidence in the future possibilities of our success. As may be seen by our Contract of Agreement, $300,000 is set aside for the benefit of the Company. Shares are $100 each. Where five or more shares are ordered at a time twenty-five per cent. may be paid down and the balance in monthly installments of like amount. Investors should understand that our stock, unlike the industrial stocks which are offered in the market, and liberally taken, is of uniform value, hence the greater advantage and safety. All moneys which accrue from said manufactures, or from the sale of lots or water privileges, and from $300,000 of stock, or any Company transactions, are to be deposited in banks as soon as received, for the benefit of stockholders. (See Section 1, Article VIII, in By-Laws.)

We are no "Boomers,"

CONSEQUENTLY *are not trying to force the sale of lots, but will not sell a single lot* until we get started with our manufacturing, as we know we can realize much more after our plant is in successful operation. We have already had applications to buy single lots, and also one application to buy a solid block, but in every instance have refused to sell before we get started in business. After that all who buy lots will be bound to erect a suitable building within a reasonable specified time. Not a single lot can be bought for speculative purposes (to stand idle for weeds to grow upon), to the detriment of our town. Many towns have been held back and seriously injured by selling a number of blocks near the business part of the town to some exacting speculator, who would hold it many years for the rise, and thereby block out numerous good enterprises which would have been of great benefit to the place. I know of such an instance in the beautiful city of Cleveland, Ohio, where a number of blocks in the best residence part of the city were held by a miserly speculator during many years; and this is only one of the many instances which occur in most cities. Such idle real estate has a tendency to depreciate the value of adjoining residence property, which would be enhanced were it occupied. We have fully decided that whatever rise there may be in our real estate the Company *shall have the benefit of.* We are not concerned but that we can sell lots as fast as is safe for the general interests of the Company, and the future welfare of our beautiful city *which is to be.* The principal cause of failure with many new towns which have started has been a desire to sell lots as fast as applications were made, before a dozen families could find employment in the town. In many cases an unsafe amount of enthusiasm was created by highly - colored advertisements, auction sales of lots, and special excursion trains, taking a large crowd of excited people, many of whom would buy lots at exorbitant and even ruinous prices, which in too many instances proved the *goal of their destruction.* They found themselves with but

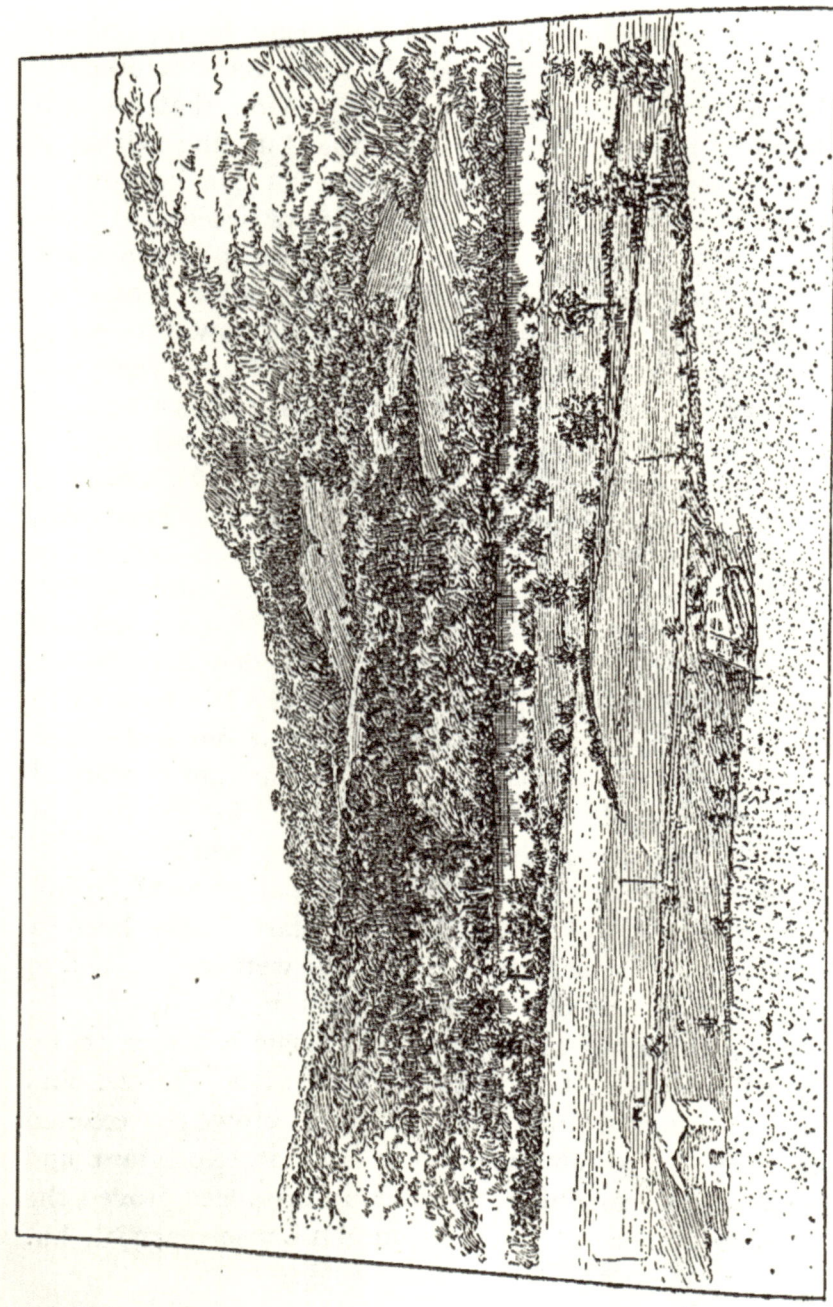

FIG. 32.—Looking North from West Oil Long City, etc.

little means and no chance to get employment to earn a dollar to help themselves, while in too many cases the heartless villains (who had, by their double-faced duplicity, absorbed what might have cost many years of hard labor) stepped out with their booty, and left their helpless victims alone in their sorrow. Realizing their situation, and as a last resort, the poor deceived people offer their lots (on which they may have made improvements) at a great sacrifice, and even then often find they can not sell. Others fall in the train of discouragement, the crash has come, and another "boom town" is recorded in the list of failures.

Whenever a town gets more population than it can give employment to, hard times and failures are sure to result. The two principal factors to build, sustain and maintain large and prosperous towns are profitable manufactures and paying mines, which enable the industrious and economical laborer to build him a comfortable home and soon become freehanded. We certainly *shall not sell lots to poor men* any faster than they can find permanent employment in our town, thereby insuring a permanent and healthy growth, with no possibility of disastrous collapse. Neither do we try to create false ideas by telling how much it will cost to grade and pave streets, lay sewers and sidewalks, and put in gas or electric fixtures, or to do a multitude of other things which may never be done. In conclusion we might say it would cost about $150,000 to do all this, which would leave us a net profit of over $1,500,000, provided we realize $1,650,000 by the sale of real estate. There have been too many of these smart and misleading calculations, made by sharpers, for the public good. It is very unsafe to make estimates of the cost of building all the public works of a city before anything is done. Such statements are calculated to influence the public mind and catch the unwary. We do nothing of the kind, as we *are not in a hurry to sell lots.* We place before investors what our Company owns, and then all may *figure for themselves.* Yet we do say that our investment is a much safer one than the great majority now on the market.

WE USE NO COLORING, in any way, in our cuts, which were made from photographs taken by the best Landscape Photographer in the city of Knoxville, Tenn. The views shown in this Prospectus are no visionary paintings, but true to life, with all the exactness of photography. I am aware that many "boom towns" have made many exaggerations, and used many borrowed views which did not belong to them. I have not allowed the engraver to "touch up" the scenes in the least; nor to add a tree, shrub or anything which can not be found in the photos. I will vouch for the truthfulness of everything found between the lids of this Prospectus. In proof of this any one who wishes to invest, who is in the least doubtful about the honesty of our views contained in this Prospectus, can, before taking any interest, see a set of 32 original photos which we have with us, which show everything true to Nature. If any one who receives this Prospectus, and can not get access to the original views we carry, wishes to satisfy himself as to their truthfulness, he can, if he so desires, have a full set of 32 landscape photos (6 x 8) sent him at the cost price of 35 cents each, $11.20 for the set, prepaid. This Prospectus will be mailed free to any one who wishes it with a view to invest. Give full name and P. O. address, plainly. Address,

L. W. MURCH,
Wolf Creek, Cocke County, Tennessee.

H. J. STODDART, Assistant General Manager.

American Oblique Manufact'g

. . . AND . . .

City Development Co.

WOLF CREEK, TENN.

OFFICERS:

L. W. MURCH, ... President and General Manager.

C. H. STEAD, ... Vice-President and Secretary.

F. R. CARVER, ... Treasurer.

H. J. STODDART, ... Assistant General Manager.

DIRECTORS:

L. W. MURCH, Wolf Creek, Tenn.

C. H. STEAD, Chicago, Ill.

F. R. CARVER, Chicago, Ill.

MAJ. W. R. SMITH, Newport, Tenn.

D. W. ALLEN, Wolf Creek, Tenn.

PLACE OF MANUFACTURE AND PRINCIPAL OFFICE:

WOLF CREEK, TENNESSEE.

BRANCH OFFICE:

110 CHAMBER OF COMMERCE, CHICAGO, ILL.

BANKERS:

THE BRITISH LINEN COMPANY'S BANK,
London and Glasgow.

THE COMMERCIAL LOAN AND TRUST CO.
Chicago.

CONTRACT OF AGREEMENT

of the

AMERICAN OBLIQUE MANUFACTURING AND CITY DEVELOPMENT COMPANY.

SECTION 1. BE IT KNOWN THAT I, LEWIS WASHINGTON MURCH, of Wolf Creek, County of Cocke, and State of Tennessee, have invented a new and useful improvement in cutting and preparing wood for ornamental and decorative purposes, for which Letters Patent for the United States were granted the fifth day of May, 1891, giving party of the first part the exclusive right to make and vend said invention throughout the United States and Territories thereof, for the term of seventeen years.

SEC. 2. NOW, THEREFORE, it is the intention of first party to commence the manufacture of the above-named invention, and to develop a town-site in conjunction with the manufacture of said patent, said site being situated at Wolf Creek, in the County of Cocke, State of Tennessee, on the waters of the French Broad River and Wolf Creek, consisting of 457 acres, more or less.

SEC. 3. Said Company shall be organized for the purpose of manufacturing, operating, and in otherwise handling or dealing with said invention by merchandising or otherwise, with the exclusive right to the States and Territories of the U. S. A., and also with the exclusive right to the development of said town-site. Said Company shall be designated as the American Oblique Manufacturing and City Development Co., and the advertising title of said Company shall be the American Oblique Mfg. & City Development Co., Manu-

86

facturers of the Celebrated Mosaic Oblique Wood Finish Furniture, Coffins and Caskets, Fancy Doors and Blinds, Moth-proof Chests, etc.

SEC. 4. First party firmly binds himself to sell to said Company all his right and title to said invention for the full term for which it was granted, also all his interest in said town-site. Said Company shall be non-assessable, with a capitalization of one million five hundred thousand dollars ($1,500,-000), divided into fifteen thousand shares of one hundred dollars ($100) each, five thousand shares of which first party will retain in his own name as a partial consideration for his invention, and interest in said town-site. First party sets aside three thousand shares to deposit in bank for the benefit of said Company. The remaining seven thousand shares first party will sell to subscribers.

SEC. 5. First party hereby guarantees to establish a twenty-five per cent. annual dividend on the manufacture of panel-pieces within five years from the commencement of said manufacture.

SEC. 6. First party hereby agrees to employ a competent photographer and engineer to take photographs and make a correct survey, from which truthful and correct maps will be made, and said maps, together with a Contract of Agreement, and By-Laws which first party has framed, will be included in a Prospectus which first party agrees to write and complete, in which he will graphically and truthfully illustrate and delineate the great natural advantages and resources of this picturesque and healthful pleasure resort and manufacturing town, backed up by an inexhaustible supply of a great variety of valuable and beautiful timber of the finest quality, and will also truthfully describe the immense water-power, etc., fully controlled within the jurisdiction of said proposed city.

First party hereby agrees to defray all expenses for doing said preliminary work (as specified in Sec. 6) free of cost to said Company.

SEC. 7. First party hereby gives said Company the use of all machines and designs which he has originated which have any relation to said invention, except three new game tables, which first party has invented, which he reserves. First party also gives said Company the use of all future machines and designs which he may invent which may have any relation to said patent, the number of which is 451,834.

SEC. 8. It is hereby agreed that second parties shall pay for patents and copyrights on all machines and designs which first party has or may originate which may have any relation to said invention.

Said machines which first party has originated will be designated as L. W. Murch's Automatic Compound Oblique Gang-log Saw-mill, and Automatic Compound Interchangeable Oblique Cabinet Machine.

The first will cut a gang of logs (more or less in number according to their size) together at once, and each time the carriage passes the logs by a gang of saws an equal number of panels will be cut from each log obliquely across the grain. By this new process beautiful panels of all sizes are cut from small, unmerchantable timber for all descriptions of fine finish. In this way stock can be cut very rapidly; more surface feet can be cut per day than can now be made from large, merchantable timber cut in the usual way parallel with the grain.

The compound interchangeable machine will cut all the various shapes to be used in said manufacture in compound form, in packs, ten or more pieces at a time. By one pass down by a gang of saws (set in various positions to cut the different sides and ends of the stock) it will cut four or more sides and ends of any desired shape (which can be cut by circular saws) *perfectly true and square*, at right angles, parallel, obliquely and vertically, on every piece of stock contained in the pack. Many classes of cabinet work can be cut in packs very rapidly, and made perfectly interchangeable, thereby saving much extra time now lost in cutting one piece at a time, and in making a number of cuts to each single piece in order to have perfect joints, which must be done on other machines. In case both ends of a draw front are to be cut at one motion by a cut-off saw, and both edges at one motion by a rip saw, it would take twenty different cuts to cut the edges and ends of ten draw fronts, ends, backs or sides, while my machine will cut the edges and ends of ten pieces at one pass down by the saws, thus reducing the cost of manufacture to a minimum and adding greatly to the manufacturers' profit. Time is money.

When getting out stock for draws, if the stock is not cut perfectly square before the draws are put together, they must be squared up after they are made in order to have them run true and get a true front. This is a costly operation, as it calls for a draw fitting machine, which, if a good one, is expensive, requires room in the factory and takes an extra man to run it. The draws also need a good deal of room, and are bulky to handle after they are put together. By cutting the stock on my machine all this trouble and expense is done away with, as the stock is cut true and square every way, so that when the draw is put together it runs perfectly true without any fitting, every piece of stock in the pack being cut exactly alike. In case the log is sawed without squaring, leaving the back on both edges of the boards,—and this kind of stock is used to work into various kinds of finish,—in order to make a perfect job with other machines the boards must be straightened on the edges before being trimmed to a perfect joint, and then only one piece at a time can be fitted to make that joint. By using my compound interchangeable machine, however, much of this trouble and expense is avoided. When boards with the bark on the edges are to be used with my machine a pack of whole length boards (as deep as a cross-cut saw can cut) are piled together and cut a proper length to be trimmed, when a pack of ten pieces (more or less in number, according to their size) are cut all together at one motion. Every piece in the pack will be found to be exactly alike and perfectly true and interchangeable, so that every piece of a kind for a thousand draws is a perfect duplicate of all the others. This applies to many different classes of work when fitted on my machine.

The machine is supplied with automatic tables, which are always closed together when cutting stock, to prevent sawdust and other matter from injuring the operator while at work. The sides and ends are closed up by adjustable shutters which, in case any adjustments are to be made on the inside of the machine, can be quickly removed, and as quickly replaced. The saws are all readily adjusted to any desired angle from the outside of the machine. The automatic form- and clamp-shafts and automatic tables quickly respond to the hand or foot of the operator; the moment the foot is removed from the foot-rest the automatic tables instantly close, and when the hand is removed from the clamp-lever handle, the change-clamp and form instantly return to their original position, thus enabling the operator to quickly and safely remove the pack which is cut and replace another to be cut. My compound saw adjustments admit of keeping the saws perfectly true vertically, and this improvement applied to cut-off and rip circular saws would admit of keeping them perfectly true also, which would insure exactly square joints. It is well-known to all who use circular saws that they are liable to get out of a true vertical position by the settling of the mandrel bearings at either end, as when the mandrel bearings have not been properly set so as to bring the saws perfectly square vertically with the top of the table ; in this case it is a very difficult task to re-adjust the mandrel bearing to set the saw perfectly square with the top of the table. With my compound saw adjustments the saw is quickly brought into the desired position, and is also quickly set so as to bring its face perfectly parallel with the line of the table and, with my adjustments, the saw mandrel is easily moved forward or back to admit of cutting different lengths of stock. Then my form and clamp shafts are kept in perfect alignment by the adjustable guy-rods.

SEC. 9. In case first party shall fail to establish said twenty-five per cent. annual dividend as herein agreed he shall forfeit his entire interest in said Company, and said interest so forfeited shall be the property of the remaining stockholders.

SEC. 10. The officers of said Company shall consist of a President, Vice-President, General Manager, Assistant General Manager, Secretary and Treasurer. L. W. Murch, the inventor and patentee, being most competent to select machinery and run the same to the best advantage in manufacturing under his process of cutting timber, and also being fully qualified to have the general supervision of his particular line of manufacture, it is deemed expedient, and for the mutual interest of all stockholders, that said Murch shall have the general supervision of the building of dams, flumes and booms, the erection of buildings and the equipment of same, and shall also have the supervision of all other business in said Company. Therefore, it is hereby agreed by the parties hereto, that said Murch shall be President, General Manager and Director in said Company until he has established said dividend; said Murch reserves the right to appoint the remaining officers and directors for the ensuing year.

SEC. 11. First party also reserves the right to give fifteen residence lots to parties who wish to build in said town, and to give seven manufacturing lots, with right to water-power and sufficent flume room in which to set water wheels to run said seven factories. The object of first party in donating said lots is to give the town a start and then to let it build itself by a natural, healthy growth *without any cost, but at a good profit*, to said Company.

First party also reserves a hotel site on which he agrees to build a commodious hotel, suitable for a pleasure and health resort, to be of handsome modern design, the interior to be finished and decorated with said oblique wood finish. The said hotel site is the same which first party has designated as Oblique Hotel on a sketch which he has drafted of said town, said town being also designated as Oblique City.

SEC. 12. The parties hereto bind themselves not to place a mortgage or lien of any description on said Company's patents, real estate, or personalty which shall in any way jeopardize the interests of any stockholder in said Company.

SEC. 13. It is hereby agreed by first and second parties, that no officers or directors in said Company shall draw any salary until after the expiration of one year from the date of its organization, but shall be allowed traveling expenses when traveling in the interests of the Company.

At the expiration of one year from the date of the organization of said Company salaries of officers shall be established and regulated by a four-fifths vote of all stockholders. The parties hereto bind themselves, their heirs, executors and assignees, to the foregoing agreement.

BY-LAWS

of the

AMERICAN OBLIQUE MANUFACTURING AND CITY DEVELOP-

MENT COMPANY.

ARTICLE I.

SECTION 1. The officers of this Company shall consist of a President, Vice-President, Secretary, Treasurer, and General Manager, all of whom shall be members of the Board of Directors.

The government of said Company shall be vested in a board of nine directors, who shall be stockholders.

SEC. 2. The term of office of the officers and directors shall be one year.

A meeting for the election of officers shall be held annually at the office of the Company, on such day as may be agreed upon and designated.

SEC. 3. All books and records of the Company shall at all times be accessible and open to the inspection of all members or their legal representatives.

ARTICLE II.

Duties of Officers.

SECTION 1.—*President.* It shall be the duty of the President to preside at all meetings of the Board of Directors, and sign all bonds, stock certificates, deeds, assignments, or other instruments made or entered into by or in behalf of this Corporation ; also to sign all checks, drafts, or orders on the treasury.

SEC. 2.—*Vice-President.* It shall be the duty of the Vice-President to perform all the duties of the President in his absence.

SEC. 3. The Secretary shall give notice of all meetings of the stockholders, either annual or special, also all meetings of the Board of Directors, quarterly or special, and keep a correct record of all transactions by the stockholders or Board of Directors in a book provided for the purpose.

He shall keep an account of all the business of the Company under the direction of the Manager and the Board of Directors.

He shall also keep a correct record of all certificates of stock, signing them only after they have been signed by the President of the Company, attaching the Corporate Seal of the Company to all documents requiring the same.

He shall, every three months, or oftener, if required by the Manager or Board of Directors, make a full, detailed statement of the business of the Company, as shown by the books kept by him (or others under him), in writing, directed to the President of the Company, which shall be submitted to the Board of Directors, and also to the stockholders at their first annual or special meeting.

The Secretary shall be the custodian of the Corporate Seal of the Company, and of all books of record, papers and documents pertaining to his office. He shall at all times keep said books of record, and all papers and documents pertaining to his office (or left in his care) in a fire-proof safe when not in actual use, said safe to be furnished by the Company.

SEC. 4.—*Treasurer.* The Treasurer shall be the custodian of the funds of the Company, and shall keep the same on deposit at a bank designated by the Board of Directors.

He shall keep a correct and full account of the same, and

shall furnish and deliver said accounts at the regular annual and all quarterly meetings of the stockholders and directors, and shall at all times honor a check, draft, or order, signed by the President and General Manager, for funds in his hands for the Company, out of any business transactions in the interest of the Company, ordered by a majority vote of the Board of Directors ; and no money shall be paid out by the Treasurer, except upon such checks, drafts, or orders.

The Treasurer shall make a report in writing as often as required by the General Manager, to the Board of Directors.

He shall execute a bond of indemnity to any amount required by the Board of Directors.

SEC. 5.—*General Manager.* It shall be the duty of the General Manager to exercise a general supervision over the affairs of the Company, to require and pass upon the reports of the Treasurer, and to cause its officers and appointees to make a full and complete report of their several departments as often as, in his judgment, the interests of the Company require the same (subject always to the direction and dictation of the Board of Directors). He shall prepare a full and complete report of all business transactions of the Company as often as required by the Board of Directors for submission to the stockholders at their annual meetings, or at any special meetings if necessary.

ARTICLE III.

Board of Directors.

SECTION 1. The Board of Directors shall meet on the first Monday of January, April, July, and October (or oftener if necessary) at the Company's office at 2 o'clock P. M.

SEC. 2. A special meeting of the Board of Directors may be called by the President, or any two directors, upon ten days' written notice, at which meeting a majority of the

Board of Directors shall constitute a quorum for the transaction of business.

Any member of the Board of Directors may appeal from the decision or the ruling of the chairman to the stockholders (from whose decision there shall be no appeal).

Sec. 3.—*Elections.* The Directors shall be elected by the stockholders at the annual meeting of the stockholders, or at any special meeting whenever there is a vacancy in the Board of Directors, each stockholder being entitled to one vote for each share of stock owned by him (or her), or legally represented by his (or her) proxy.

ARTICLE IV.
Certificates of Stock.

Section 1. The capital stock of this Company shall be $1,500,000, divided into 15,000 shares of $100 each.

Sec. 2. Bound books of certificates of stock, of the form and tenor determined by the Board of Directors, shall be placed in the custody of the Secretary, and all certificates of stock shall be signed by the President and Secretary under the corporate seal of the Company.

Sec. 3. Transfers of certificates of stock shall be made only on the books of the Company, either in person, or by attorney holding power of attorney in fact, which power of attorney shall be satisfactorily identified by the Secretary. The possession of stock can not be regarded as evidence of ownership, unless it reasonably appears that said certificates of stock were duly assigned or legally transferred to the holder of the same.

ARTICLE V.
Stockholders.

Section 1. The regular annual meeting of the stockholders of this Company shall be called on the first Tuesday of January of each year at 2 o'clock P. M.

The books of the Company shall be closed 10 days before such meeting.

Holders of certificates of stock may vote in person or by proxy, all proxies to be submitted and passed upon before the stockholders shall transact business. Each share to represent one vote in all business transacted at the stockholders' meeting; such meeting to be held in the office of the Company.

The stock-book to be closed to the transfer of stock 10 days previous to the date of such meeting.

The stockholders shall have the power at any annual, quarterly or special meeting, to retire any officer or director from active service and place another in his stead, whenever they shall deem it for the best good of the Company.

SEC. 2. All business transactions in this Company shall be conducted and controlled by a four-fifths vote, and each stockholder shall have the right to vote in person or by proxy in all elections, and to cast one ballot for each share of stock held by him or her.

All special meetings of the stockholders to be called and held as specified by the statutes of the State in which the principal office of this Company is located.

ARTICLE VI.

Debts.

SECTION 1. No debt shall be contracted for the Company, except by the order of the Board of Directors representing a four-fifths vote of stock.

ARTICLE VII.

Mortgages and Liens.

SECTION 1. No mortgages or liens shall ever be placed on any part of this Company's patents, real estate or personalty, which shall in any way jeopardize the interests of any stockholders.

ARTICLE VIII.
Dividends.

SECTION 1. Dividends shall be made semi-annually from the funds in the hands of the Treasurer that shall appear as excess of receipts over disbursements.

SEC. 2. Each and every stockholder shall receive their just and rightful dividend from all moneys which may accrue from all business transactions, by merchandising or otherwise, and shall receive said dividend semi-annually, the first day of June and December in each year.

SEC. 3. All moneys which shall accrue to this Company from the sale of said $300,000 of stock, or from the sale of lots or water privileges, or from said manufacture by merchandising or otherwise, shall (as soon as received) be deposited in this Company's banks, either in Chicago, Ill., or London, England (said banks being designated in the Company's Prospectus), and no part of said moneys so deposited shall be drawn from said deposit except for the benefit of said Company, and then only by an order from the General Manager, which shall be countersigned by the President and Secretary. If any officer, director or stockholder in this Company shall be proven to have tampered in the least with the funds of the Company he shall forfeit his entire interest in said Company without resort to law in any way.

ARTICLE IX.
Prohibitions and Restrictions.

SECTION 1. All stockholders (in this Company), their heirs, executors and assignees are hereby bound never to harbor, encourage, or allow any description of nuisances or immoral practices on, in, or about said Company's premises or buildings, or on, in, or around any real estate or personalty which they at present own, or may in the future acquire within the jurisdiction of the extreme limits of a town site on which said Company proposes to build a city, said city to be designated as "Oblique City," and situated in the County of Cocke, and State of Tennessee, on the waters of the French Broad River and Wolf Creek.

SEC. 2. All stockholders (in this Company), their heirs, executors and assignees, are hereby bound not to build, or allow to be built, any building of any description for immoral practices, such as houses of ill-fame, or for gambling of any description, or for keeping or selling any kind of intoxicating liquors, in any way or form, or to be used as opium dens in any way or form, or for keeping, introducing, selling or posting obscene literature, pictures, photographs, prints, or vulgar or indecent statuary of any description, or for shooting galleries of any description, or to encourage or allow dog-fighting, cock-fighting or prize-fighting of any kind, nor to allow any kind of cruelty to persons, birds or animals in any way or form, on any part of said Company's premises, or in, on, or about any real estate or personal property within the extreme limits of said proposed city, or in, on, or around any additions which may at any time in the future be made or added to said city.

SEC. 3. All stockholders in said Company are hereby bound (and pledge themselves, their heirs, executors and assignees) to prevent, to the best of their ability, all of the above-named nuisances and immoral practices. If any person or persons, whomsoever, shall at any time attempt, in any way or form, to perpetrate, encourage, introduce, locate, or tolerate any of the above-named nuisances, or immoral practices, on, in, or around said Company's premises, or in, on, or about said Company's buildings, or in, on, or around any real estate or personalty within the extreme limits of said proposed city, or in, on, or around any addition which may in the future be made or added to said city, then all stockholders in said Company, and also their heirs, executors, and assignees, shall immediately and at once, banish and destroy all such nuisances and immoral practices. In case of failure to comply with these agreements and requirements, they shall be guilty of a misdemeanor and shall be punished to the extreme penalty of the law.

SEC. 4. All deeds, contracts, and every other conveyance, or lease of real estate, or personalty given by said Company, shall contain a provision forbidding all of the above-named nuisances and immoral practices, and a verbatim copy of the above-named prohibitions and restrictions shall be fully and truthfully embraced in each and all of the above-named instruments whenever conveyances are made by assignor to assignee. None of the above-named instruments shall be valid unless they contain a verbatim copy of Sections 1, 2, and 3, of Article IX, as laid down in these By-Laws.

ARTICLE X.
Provisions for Public Benefit.

SECTION 1. A provision is hereby made that ten per cent. of all moneys received from the sale of said three thousand shares of stock (which first party has set aside in his Contract of Agreement with the American Oblique Manufacturing and City Development Company) shall be used as follows: When the ten per cent. of receipts from the sale of said stock shall amount to five thousand dollars ($5,000), it shall be used to build a suitable building, three stories high, for the following purposes: The first floor for a school room and church, until a suitable church can be built, and the second and third floors for Masonic and Odd Fellows Halls, and also for other public and private uses. The remainder of said ten per cent. of receipts shall be used to keep said building in repair, and also to further and promote such needed improvements in said proposed city as shall, from time to time, be deemed advisable for the mutual interests of all concerned. All improvements to be made and all moneys to be used in the various improvements shall be conducted and controlled by a four-fifths vote of all stockholders in said Company.

SEC. 2. An annual tax of one mill on the dollar shall be levied on all real estate and personalty in said city, to establish and maintain a Public Library, and said tax shall be perpetual to add to, improve, and maintain said library. No literature of a pernicious nature shall ever be kept in same. Its control and management shall be vested in a Board of Trustees, consisting of five members, who shall be elected by a majority of all the voters in said city. Said board shall be elected at the annual meeting of the officers of said library, consisting of President, Vice-President, Secretary, Treasurer and Librarian. Officers of said board shall hold their offices until their successors are elected and qualified.

ARTICLE XI.

Amendments.

SECTION. 1. These prohibitions and provisions shall forever remain a fixture in these By-Laws, and shall be revised by the stockholders only, and then upon a ten days' notice to the stockholders of the amendment to be made, which shall be done by a four-fifths vote of stock.

Maj. R. C. McCalla, Civil Engineer.

Opinion of Maj. R. C. McCalla, Civil Engineer, Tuscaloosa, Alabama.

WOLF CREEK, TENN., *June 15, 1893.*

L. W. MURCH, Esq.

DEAR SIR : In answer to your request, I beg to hand you my opinion of Wolf Creek, or "Oblique City," for manufacturing and health resort purposes, as follows, viz. : In the first place you have explained to me the advantages you have in the patented devices for the sawing of timber, of all sizes, diagonally across the grain, which is to be used for the extensive manufacture of the most unique and delicately penciled furniture, and which you believe can be shipped to all of the cultivated nations. You have explained that your patents in this country and Europe, and especially in Australia, will give you a monopoly of all manufactured goods made possible through these peculiar inventions. If these things be so, then you are in command of a situation that is calculated to develop a wonderful industry, for you purpose to utilize your process for the ornamentation of buildings, railway cars, street railway cars, steamboats, wooden vessels, steamships, and every kind of ornamentation where wood is the essential material. To my mind it appears that the demand for the work made possible by your inventions may exceed your best efforts to supply it.

Impressed, as I now am, that your invention is all that you claim for it, and that you propose to test it at Oblique City, on a large scale, it will not, perhaps, be amiss that I now undertake to give a simple statement as to what Oblique City is, and where it is, and its special fitness for comfortably locating the people who are expected to come here and embark in the labors of this novel industrial town. Well, it has been my privilege to have been familiar with this immediate locality for many years—say all along, at short intervals, since 1858 or 1859, about 34 years.

It is a most beautiful spot, affording a picture of natural scenery which always enchanted me. When my health would become impaired in the malarial districts of the South, it was my first desire to go to Wolf Ceeek, which always greatly improved, or entirely restored, me.

103

On such occasions it was occasionally suggested to friends, "we must have a nice town at Wolf Creek for the accommodation of summer visitors, and for manufacturing purposes." Now I would suggest that we enlarge on this idea; let us put in place the machinery you have in view, and every body to come from the East and the West, and the North, and the South, and our friends across the seas.

Many years ago the distinguished engineer who marked out the way for a railroad from Charleston, South Carolina, to Cincinnati, Ohio, said in his able report: "And now, having attained the summit of the Blue Ridge, the plains of East Tennessee lie stretched out before us, temptingly inviting the invasion of the iron horse, a country whose marvelous resources in iron, coal, timber, water-power and agricultural resources invite to increased efforts in consummating the grand project; and the goddess of health presides and smiles over every square mile of this magnificent panorama."

That was written 56 years ago, but the project was not fully opened until about a year ago, when the last tracks were put upon the Morristown and Cumberland Gap Railroad, so that these wonderful resources are still here in all their virgin purity, as it were. The French Broad River is a remarkable stream, and has its source in the Blue Ridge Mountains. It has always reminded me of a great spring heading in the mountains, accumulating increased and perennial volume from a thousand rivulets and several large tributaries.

The distance from Wolf Creek to the head springs of this beautiful river, I estimate at 80 to 90 miles, and the great drainage basin of the French Broad above your city is to furnish the timber for your mills here, and it consists of many varieties in practically inexhaustible quantities. The water power of the French Broad between this and Asheville is immense. The distance is about 50 miles, every mile of which would furnish power for one or more cotton or other factories, situated in close proximity to the cotton fields of the Carolinas.

But there is no place between this and Asheville where could be founded a manufacturing city and health resort such as could be built at Wolf Creek or Oblique City. This is unquestionably the place for the big town of the French Broad, west of Asheville, N. C. But the day is not far distant, perhaps, when this entire distance of 50 miles shall be studded with cotton manufacturing in its various phases. Such was my opinion 30 years ago, and I can conceive of no reason to-day why I should change it. The uniformly healthful climate, the moderate temperature, the immense timber, stone, iron and other mineral resources, the abundant water-power occurring at intervals of every half mile, the spirit of health which presides over all, and its close proximity to the cotton fields of the Carolinas certainly point to it as the great manufacturing site of East Tennessee, and perhaps the greatest in the South. Therefore, I believe that you have displayed fine judgment in making the selection you have for your manufacturing site.

It is proper to state that I have just completed the survey and made a personal reconnoisance, and prepared your maps from actual survey and close observations. The dam already located is to be 11 feet high, and will furnish a water power estimated at 2,691 horse-power. Another dam 4,300 feet above this dam is estimated to be 8 feet high, and is to accommodate the plant for generating the electricity to be used in general mechanical operations. Thirty-two hundred feet above this affords a fine site for another dam, but the grounds above, at present, are in the hands of other parties. Therefore, I will not count it now; at or near the lower end of your holding you have another dam site, which will furnish a power of 18 feet vertical, estimated from actual level as determined for the dam of 11 feet above referred to. The estimated capacity for building sites I have fixed as follows, viz. : 859 residence lots, comfortably housing 4,295 persons ; 421 elevated residence lots, sheltering 2,105 people, and 17 large elevated residence lots, nicely accommodating 170 souls. This is the ground-floor estimate, so each person may form his own opinion as to its capacity for population as cities are ordinarily built. The lots generally are 50 x 125 feet, the streets 40 feet wide. Two avenues will be respectively 100 and 75 feet in width. There will be 163 business lots 25 x 125 feet.

Everything in this city will be parallel to the railroad, which has been taken as the base.

The seventeen large elevated residence lots are very nicely located, with several acres each, and are set apart for the accommodation of gentlemen of large means, who wish plenty of comfort, much ease, and admirable resources for pleasure, but who still have a taste for the hum of industry and the whirl of machinery. For all such this unique city in the mountains and its suburbs will afford a very inviting field.

Paint Rock, 4½ miles above you, is the point where the French Broad cuts through the Great Smoky Mountains, and on the south of Wolf Creek it is only a rise of 8 miles to the top of this great range, hence the delightful summer climate of Oblique City, and hence the opportunities for the multiplied mountain excursions which always afford so much pleasure to excursionists, tourists, and pleasure and health seekers.

I may refer to the great iron and coal center of Alabama,—Birmingham,—and hint at its phenomenal growth in the last decade, and call attention to the fact that only about 20 years ago its first business house was erected. Now it has a population, city and suburbs, variously estimated at from 30,000 to 50,000 inhabitants.

This marvelous growth is emphatically due to her manufacturing efforts. Harriman, in the Chattanooga district, realized $604,000 for 574 lots in her first auction sale, and though the infant town is lagging in this great financial pressure, yet many believe in her future as a live manufacturing centre. Middleborough, Ky., is a notable example of what energy and push and money can do, but it, too, is passing through the same depressing influences which have checked the growth of Birmingham and Harriman.

Each in its place furnishes a good object lesson to those who are just about to embark in similar enterprises, i. e., "Trust in Providence, but keep your powder dry." Build fast as you please, but surely and wisely; put everything into machinery and keep it moving; put energetic, honest business men at the helm, and indulge in nothing fanciful until you have everything on a sound mechanical basis ; then it will be soon enough to spend money for beautifying your city.

In conclusion I beg to say that I have been for the last three weeks an observer of your matchless energy, your great sincerity, and seeming honesty of purpose, and have come to the conclusion that these are desirable gifts connected with your great industry, especially pointing to you as the one best calculated to lead in this good undertaking ; and my best wishes go with you in your efforts to organize the Company.

Yours truly,

R. C. McCALLA,

Civil Engineer.

Vouchers for Major R. C. McCalla.

KNOXVILLE, *June 17, 1893.*

L. W. MURCH, Esq., Wolf Creek, Tenn.

MY DEAR SIR: Replying to your favor of 12th inst., would say that I have known Maj. R. C. McCalla for the past 12 years, he having been associated with me as chief engineer in charge of construction of the Knoxville & Ohio R. R. extension under my control, and on other important work, covering a period of several years. It may be proper to add that Maj. McCalla has been recognized as one of the leading civil engineers in this country for many years past.

His character as a citizen is above question, commanding, as he does, and always has done, the respect of every one.

Any official report that he may make of any question that he may be called upon to investigate would be entitled to every confidence ; more particularly so, being, as he is, a very cool, careful and conservative man, whose judgment in matters of business can be safely relied upon and whose professional opinion would have a tendency to induce one to look carefully into any proposed investment that met with his approval.

Personally, I regard Maj. McCalla as one of the most scrupulously correct gentlemen in all the relations of life that I have ever known.

I am, very respectfully, your obedient servant,

F. K. HUGER,
Supt. E. T. V. & G. Ry. Co.

TUSCALOOSA, ALA., *June 20, 1893.*

Mr. L. W. MURCH, Wolf Creek, Tenn.

DEAR SIR : Your letter of some days ago is received. In answer to your interrogations, taking them in the order in which they come, I will state :—

1st. That I know Maj. R. C. McCalla, and have known him for more than twenty years.

2d. His reputation in Alabama, as a Civil Engineer, is first rate. I don't know how he rates out of Alabama, as I never heard his reputation discussed outside of Alabama.

3d. His general character is as good as any man I ever knew, in every respect.

4th. The fullest confidence would be given any statement or report, official, or otherwise, that Maj. McCalla might make, by those who know him in Alabama, I think. I don't know any person who is thoroughly acquainted with him who hasn't implicit confidence in his high character and integrity.

5th. He is remarkable for his deliberation and cool judgment. His

Maj. W. R. Smith, Director.

enthusiasm never causes him to lose his deliberate judgment. His judgment is remarkable for its soundness.

6th. In his daily life, at home, he has always seemed to be blameless, and his word is regarded as good as his bond with every one in this community, so far as I have ever heard. In fact, I have not in all my experience met many men who have impressed me with as much favor as Maj. McCalla, for truth and uprightness of character.

7th. Such is my confidence in the high character and sound judgment of Maj. McCalla, that his recommendation of any business enterprise would strengthen my confidence in its merits.

I think nineteen out of twenty of the best men in the county would answer your questions in a way not less commendatory of the character of Maj. McCalla, than I have done above.

Very respectfully,
A. C. HARGROVE,
Ex-President of the Senate of Alabama, and Professor of Law in the University of Alabama.

Opinion of Maj. W. R. Smith, of Newport, Tennessee.

NEWPORT, TENN., *June 12, 1893.*

To whom it may concern:

Having known the bearer of this (Mr. L. W. Murch) intimately for some length of time, it affords me pleasure to recommend him to the favorable consideration of those with whom he may come in contact, or desire to establish business relations.

I have ever found him a man of strict veracity, unimpeachable integrity, honorable and just in his dealings, and one who would scorn to mislead even the humblest.

Possessed of superior talent as an inventor, he also has the executive ability to apply what he invents, and turn it to the use for which it was intended.

Of indomitable energy, great industry and fixedness of purpose, he is eminently qualified to successfully manage and conduct such an enterprise as that to which he is now devoting his time and energies.

Having recently purchased at Wolf Creek, Cocke County, Tennessee, a town site, comprising about 500 acres, he proposes to establish there a manufacturing city, and also a health and pleasure resort, for which it is so admirably adapted.

His first step will be the putting in of a plant to manufacture, under the new process discovered by himself (and upon which he has a monopoly for the United States, Great Britain, Canada and Australia). He will work the various timbers into lumber and rare ornamental work of a beauty heretofore unknown, and which needs only to be seen to be appreciated.

In the choice of Wolf Creek for his enterprise, Mr. Murch displayed that fine mechanical judgment for which he is noted, and showed a high appreciation of the "fitness of things." By the purchase of that property he got just what he needed—he got a big mountain river, which rushing down from a high elevation dashes onward the entire length of the property, furnishing water-power sufficient to turn the wheels of multiplied machinery. He got a location in the midst of dense, extensive forests of valuable timber, equal to the demands for generations to come.

He purchased railway and water transportation for bringing in these timbers and carrying out to the markets of the world their products. He got possession of the key point which commands one of the most important mineral belts of Cocke County, and which is the natural trading and shipping depot for a large industrial district of country capable of supporting much population, and of richly remunerating the industrious tiller of the soil by its luxuriant grasses, choice vegetables and delicious fruits.

Such are some of the solid advantages secured by Mr. Murch when he wisely purchased Wolf Creek; but with these, he, too, got a town site which, for romantic beauty, natural fitness and great possibilities is rarely equaled.

He got a widely known, highly valued health and pleasure resort, with its purest air, its springs of chalybeate, sulphur and free-stone waters, its mountain and water scenery, its carriage ways along the river side and into the recesses of the great mountain ranges, a place where Nature's own fixed laws placed a quarantine upon disease, and says to the invalid, "be thou whole"; to the weak and feeble, "receive strength." Wolf Creek opens wide her gates and invites the investor, the money maker, the man of means burdened with the cares of business and longing for retirement and peaceful rest; to all she says, come and see for yourself the opportunities and possibilities offered by me.   Very respectfully,

W. R. SMITH,
Newport, Cocke County, Tennessee.

110

Vouchers for Maj. W. R. Smith.

To whom it may concern: NEWPORT, TENN., *June 13, 1893.*

We, the undersigned, who know personally W. R. Smith, the author of the enclosed letter recommending L. W. Murch, beg to say that we know him to be a gentleman to be relied upon when he makes a statement.

He has lived in this county for a great number of years, and we know of no man who, possesses the respect and confidence of the people to a greater extent than he does, and who would be farther from making an untruthful statement.

> C. B. MIMS, POSTMASTER.
> W. O. MIMS, ATTORNEY.
> W. J. McSWEEN, ATTORNEY.
> ALLEN G. BRYANT, REG. DEEDS, Cocke County, Tenn.
> J. W. STEWART, JUSTICE, Cocke County, Tenn.
> W. H. PENLAND, CLERK CO. COURT.
> JNO. R. SHULTZ, CLERK CHANCERY COURT.
> REV. JAS. I. CASH.
> S. A. BURNETT, ASSISTANT CASHIER COCKE COUNTY M. & P. BANK.

Opinion of Messrs. Palmer and Corway.

NEWPORT, TENN., *June 13, 1893.*

Mr. L. W. MURCH, Wolf Creek, Tenn.

DEAR SIR : Yours received and contents noted ; in reply, will say that I will be glad to superintend your fine furniture department. In regard to Mr. Corway, will say, he is a fine workman, and a man of good mechanical judgment. In fact I consider him one of the best mechanics, and he says you can depend on him to start and stay with you at Wolf Creek as soon as you get ready for him.

Like myself, he says your invention is a *valuable one*, and sure to be in great demand when once it is placed upon the market.

He thinks, as I do, that as your way of cutting timber is entirely new you will have a valuable monopoly when you get your two new machines patented, for they will surely renew the life of your patent for

CHARLES PALMER, Company's Superintendent of Fine Furniture Department.

cutting timber obliquely, and with your two new machines you can do the work much quicker and cheaper than it can be done on any machine now in use.

In fact it is impossible to cut timber your way and give the least margin of profit without your gang-log saw-mill, and but a small profit could be realized in working your stock into the various branches which you propose to without your compound interchangeable machine. It certainly is a great labor saver, doing work so rapidly and making such perfect joints ; in fact, it is invaluable to furniture manufacturers throughout the world, as so many different shapes can be cut upon it so rapidly, which will reduce the cost of manufacture to a minimum, which will certainly leave a big margin of profit, as you get your stock out of small, unmarketable timber, of which the country is full.

Your invention is, indeed, *a valuable one, as it is invaluable* wherever the beauty of wood is called for. We both join in wishing you much success and are only *too anxious* to pitch our tents at " Oblique City " ; that is, if you think we can " fill the bill." Yours truly,

CHAS. PALMER.

P. S.—They are *just wild* over the table I sent to Arkansas. Small stock cut your way is nicely adapted for this kind of work, as well as many others.

Opinion of W. E. Singleton, Photographer.

KNOXVILLE, TENN., *July 18, 1893.*

Mr. L. W. MURCH, Washington, D. C.

DEAR SIR : Yours containing check for $11.50 to pay for photos. just received. Many thanks for your order. All future orders shall receive prompt attention, and will guarantee satisfaction in every way. It gives me pleasure to state that yours are the finest lot of landscape views I have ever taken at any new town, and that is saying considerable, as I have done much work in the South, as I have taken views at Middlesborough, Harriman, Coal Creek, Jelico, Elk Valley, and many other important town sites.

With your very desirable attractions at Wolf Creek, more particularly fine scenery, high altitude, healthful climate, and pure, health-giving waters, you are bound to (in the near future) make one of the most desirable health and pleasure resorts in the South. Many of our people in Knoxville, as well as all over the South, can testify to the big picnics and social gatherings we have enjoyed at Wolf Creek.

Many a Knoxville citizen looks forward with anticipated pleasure to our annual gatherings at Wolf Creek, "Oblique City."

When you get the hotel which you contemplate building at Wolf Creek, you are bound to have it filled with guests, as many who could not be accommodated in the past are sure to come to this delightful place to recuperate, and get a season of rest and pleasurable enjoyment. I think your head is level in not pushing the sale of lots as Harriman did, as you are sure to sell lots quite fast enough when you get started, and then, as you say, the Company will get the full benefit of whatever rise there may be on real estate. I am highly satisfied with my little investment, and hope to be able to take more stock in a few months. I could not get away with the excursion which went to Wolf Creek for their annual outing the other day, but understand they had a very enjoyable time.

Awaiting further orders, and wishing you every success imaginable, I am, dear sir, Very respectfully,

W. E. SINGLETON.

Opinion of Benton J. Hall, Ex=Commissioner of Patents.

BENTON J. HALL, PATENT ATTORNEY,
Monadnock Building,
CHICAGO.

CHICAGO, ILLINOIS, *July 22, 1893.*

L. W. MURCH, Wolf Creek, Tenn.

DEAR SIR : I beg to say that I have examined your plans and drawings for your inventions in improvements in machines for sawing timber obliquely into panels, and also for cutting the panels into any desired form or shape. While you have not fully worked out all the details of the oblique sawing machine, I am satisfied you have the full conception of a very novel and useful machine, and that there will be no difficulty in completing the simple details and making it operative and successful.

The machine for forming or cutting the panels as shown is complete in design and drawing, and I have no doubt will be operative and useful. These two machines are very important, in that they reinforce your patent heretofore issued upon the process or method of cutting timber obliquely into panels. They will, when perfected and patented, practically prolong the life of your first patent, for the reason that

W. E. Singleton, Company's Photographer.

these machines, when patented, put it beyond the power of others to obliquely cut timber into panels as you can, and in consequence there can be no real competition in the work.

Yours very truly,

BENTON J. HALL,
Late U. S. Commissioner of Patents.

Opinion of Messrs. Gass & Bassford.

GASS & BASSFORD,
612 First National Bank Building,
CHICAGO.
Cable Address, "Sago."

CHICAGO, ILLINOIS, *July 22, 1893.*

Mr. L. W. MURCH, Wolf Creek, Tenn.

DEAR SIR: During our business negotiations the past winter and spring we have taken great interest in the examination of the patent held by you for the construction of panels by the oblique sawing of timber, and it is our opinion that the plans and drawings of the machinery designed by you to produce these panels in large quantity and exact duplication of size will enable you to form a plant by which you can turn these panels out at a cost that is less than is possible by any other known process, thus giving you absolute command of the market, and obviating the possibility of successful competition.

Congratulating you on the financial success which this should assure you, we beg to remain,

Yours very respectfully,

GASS & BASSFORD.

Opinion of C. H. Stead.

C. H. STEAD, REAL ESTATE AND LOANS,
1110 Chamber Commerce, Chicago.

CHICAGO, ILLINOIS, *July 21, 1893.*

Mr. L. W. MURCH, Newport, Tenn.

DEAR SIR: Referring to your favor of recent date in regard to the value of lots in the city you are about to develop, comparing them with others in towns similarly situated, they should sell on an average of

$1,000 apiece. It is my opinion that you can divide the land into 1,700 to 2,000 lots.

In most all towns and cities in the United States that have a population of 5,000 to 10,000, lots sell at from $10 to $200 per front foot. Thus, lots of regular size, 25 x 125 feet, sell from $250 to $5,000 apiece. In most all of these places there is an abundance of ground on the outskirts to subdivide into lots, which would have a tendency to make lower prices. In the case of your city it is entirely different, as it is nestled in the valley and your Company owns all the land that can be utilized for building purposes. I think there is no possible doubt but your land after being divided into lots and sold will net $1,500,000 after paying all expenses. After having a number of years' experience in the real estate business, I think you can base your calculations to a large degree upon the above facts.

Yours very truly,
C. H. STEAD.
Real Estate and Loans, Chicago, Ill.

Testimonials from Leading Men of Newport, Tenn.

NEWPORT, TENN., *July 15, 1893.*

To whom it may concern:

We, the undersigned, citizens of Newport, Tennessee, having seen and carefully examined specimens of lumber produced by Mr. Lewis Washington Murch under the new process of sawing timber discovered and patented by him, do heartily approve the same, and unhesitatingly recommend his invention to all who admire the beautiful and appreciate the profitable and the useful.

D. A. MIMS, CASHIER M. & P. BANK.

S. A. BURNETT, ASS'T CASHIER M. & P. BANK.

W. H. JONES, ATTORNEY.

JNO. R. SHUTT, CLERK AND MASTER.

C. B. MIMS, POSTMASTER.

DEATON & WILLIS, FURNITURE.

H. N. KATE, ATTORNEY-AT-LAW.

REV. JAS. I. CASH.

INDEX

HISTORICAL REPRINT

Cross Mountain Books

In addition to *Oblique City*, enjoy *Ada's Journal, Charley's Novel,* and these forthcoming titles in The Pecks of Mossy Creek series.

Ada's Journal: The Civil War Era Journal and Letters of Emma Peck

Ada's Journal provides a window into history. Ada Louise Peck was a well-loved little girl (and Charley Peck's sister) who traveled back and forth between Mossy Creek, Tennessee and East Carroll Parish, Louisiana, starting in 1853. She experienced trials, health problems, and travel by railroad, steamboat, and stagecoach. This journal, recorded from Ada's perspective by her mom Emma, records the first two years of her short life. Edited by Andy Peck, over 70 photographs, maps, and historical references bring this true story to life in a powerful way. Journey with little Ada on a Mississippi River steamboat; keep your hands inside the train as you pass through the half-mile Cumberland Mountain Tunnel on the East Tennessee and Georgia Railroad; and enjoy the mountain hospitality at the Wolf Creek Inn as Ada visits with Mrs. Emma Allen, Peck family friend and hostess to hundreds along the French Broad River.

ISBN 9781955121002 (pbk) | ISBN 9781955121019 (hardcover)

ISBN 9781955121026 (ebook)

Charley's Novel: Mary Anderson and Peacock the Mineralogist, the Bad Luck of a Young Southern Girl

Written in 1879, and set in Eastern Tennessee, North Carolina, Virginia, and West Virginia, this epic tale shares the compelling story of Mary Anderson, a wealthy young southern girl enchanted by the reputable and knowledgeable Mr. Peacock. Mary's father, Mr. Anderson, is eager to place his daughter and family in a better position with such a profitable union. But what if the allure of Peacock's beautiful feathers turns into a case of fatal attraction? Honeymoon excitement suddenly turns to tragedy in the mountains of North Carolina, and life will never be the same for Mary and her family. How will she handle her position as a refined young woman, wife, and mother, as she endures the abuse of the stranger, Mr. Peacock? Will Peacock fulfill his many promises? Will Mary fight her way to independence? Is there hope for her and her little boy?

ISBN 9781955121163 (pbk) | ISBN 9781955121170 (hardcover)

ISBN 9781955121187 (ebook)

Cross Mountain Books ™
www.crossmountainbooks.com/charley

Sawbones: The Life and Times of Dr. Isham Talbot Peck

Between 1874 and 1886, Dr. Isham Peck (Charley's father, and grandson of Adam Peck, Sr., founder of Mossy Creek) wrote letters to the editor of *The Morristown Gazette* under the pen name Sawbones, and people wrote to him as well. *Sawbones* takes you on a deep dive into life in East Tennessee and Northeastern Louisiana during the years of Reconstruction after the Civil War and beyond. *Sawbones* expresses his thoughts on politics, agriculture, church, friendship, and fishing. Author/Editor Andy Peck includes the history of Isham Peck and family, including what is known about his pre-Civil War service in the U.S. Army as a surgeon. Allow yourself to be transported to places like Wolf Creek, Tennessee as the author includes a series of videos recorded at places where Isham and family lived. *Sawbones* is a journey worth experiencing!

ISBN 9781955121088 (pbk) | ISBN 9781955121095 (hardcover)

Cross Mountain Books
www.crossmountainbooks.com

He Loved the Folks: Dr. Edward Jerome Peck of Hot Springs, North Carolina by Andy Peck

In *He Loved the Folks*, learn how this doctor from Wolf Creek, Tennessee gently influenced the entire area around Hot Springs, North Carolina for good by his steady, faithful, medical care. Dr. Ed Peck (son of Dr. Isham Talbot Peck) was so loved at the time of his death, that the community came together and erected a monument to honor his life and love. He doctored Jane (Hicks) Gentry, the Appalachian folklorist and singer, and served important Hot Springs institutions including the Dorland Institute, Mountain Park Hotel, and the Southern Railway Surgeons Association. In *He Loved the Folks*, you will catch a glimpse as to why this man was so loved by the Hot Springs community, as he dedicated his life to them.

ISBN 9781955121040 (pbk) | ISBN 9781955121057 (hardcover)

Cross Mountain Books
www.crossmountainbooks.com